Praise for Je

INVISIBLE AMERICANS

"A useful book that reveals what might be considered a secret shame but that is hiding in plain sight."
—*Kirkus Reviews*

"Compelling. . . . Madrick addresses a systemic problem with a simple solution. His argument will appeal to those who champion economic policy change that centers the child." —Angela Forret, *Library Journal*

"Thoroughly researched. . . . Madrick's research shows that current efforts are woefully inadequate, and he makes a reasonable plea for change."
—Kathleen McBroom, *Booklist*

"*Invisible Americans* provides a devastating portrait of the nature and consequences of child poverty in the United States. Madrick demonstrates that these worrisome poverty rates are the result of multiple policy failures—failures that result, in turn, from choices that Americans have made. Madrick explains, with passion and precision, that the necessary policy instruments are known and tested."
—Janet C. Gornick, author of *Families That Work*

"Madrick systematically builds the case for a universal monthly allowance for children that will dramatically reduce child poverty. He offers both a comprehensive view of the history of child poverty in our nation and a glimpse of where we may be headed."

—David Harris, president of
Children's Research and Education Institute

"In *Invisible Americans*, Jeff Madrick shines invaluable light on a much-neglected crisis: the more than one in five children—some thirteen million children— who live in poverty in the world's wealthiest nation. Madrick explains how this crisis has stunted millions of children and shows how the United States has fallen woefully short of its promise of equal opportunity. Madrick makes devastatingly clear that America's child poverty problem is a moral disgrace. Concise, compelling, and urgent, *Invisible Americans* concludes with some smart ideas on how to quickly reduce child poverty."

—Steven Greenhouse, author of
Beaten Down, Worked Up

"Jeff Madrick gives an excellent account of the contours and consequences of child poverty in the United States, as well as the failed social policies of the last three decades that have done little to address this problem. He also makes a powerful argument for the simplest possible solution, giving poor families money. A very timely and useful book."

—Dean Baker, author of *Rigged*

JEFF MADRICK

INVISIBLE AMERICANS

Jeff Madrick, a former economics columnist for *Harper's Magazine* and *The New York Times,* is a regular contributor to *The New York Review of Books* and *The Nation* and editor of *Challenge Magazine.* He is visiting professor of humanities at The Cooper Union, director of the Bernard L. Schwartz Rediscovering Government Initiative, and a fellow at The Century Foundation. His books include *Seven Bad Ideas, Age of Greed, The End of Affluence,* and *Taking America.* He has also written for *The Washington Post,* the *Los Angeles Times, Institutional Investor, The Nation, The American Prospect, The Boston Globe,* and *Newsday.* He lives in New York City.

www.jeffmadrick.com

ALSO BY JEFF MADRICK

*Seven Bad Ideas: How Mainstream Economists
Have Damaged America and the World*

*Age of Greed: The Triumph of Finance and
the Decline of America, 1970 to the Present*

The Case for Big Government

*Why Economies Grow: The Forces That Shape
Prosperity and How to Get Them Working Again*

*The End of Affluence: The Causes and
Consequences of America's Economic Dilemma*

*Taking America: How We Got from
the First Hostile Takeover to Megamergers,
Corporate Raiding and Scandal*

*Unconventional Wisdom: Alternative Perspectives
on the New Economy* (editor)

INVISIBLE AMERICANS

THE TRAGIC COST OF CHILD POVERTY

JEFF MADRICK

VINTAGE BOOKS

A DIVISION OF PENGUIN RANDOM HOUSE LLC

NEW YORK

The Library of Congress has cataloged the Knopf edition as follows:
Name: Madrick, Jeffrey G., author.
Title: Invisible Americans : the tragic cost of child poverty / Jeff Madrick.
Description: First Edition. | New York : Alfred A. Knopf, 2020. |
Includes bibliographical references (pages 175–218) and index.
Identifiers: LCCN 2019022606
Subjects: LCSH: Poor children—United States—Social conditions. |
Poverty—United States. | Child welfare—United States.
Classification: LCC HV741 .M3326 2020 | DDC 362.7086/9420973—dc23
LC record available at https://lccn.loc.gov/2019022606

Vintage Books Trade Paperback ISBN: 978-1-101-97405-6
eBook ISBN: 978-0-451-49419-1

Author photograph © Michael Lionstar
Book design by Soonyoung Kwon

www.vintagebooks.com

To the dozens of researchers
who dedicate their lives to studying
the causes and consequences of child poverty

And to my wife, Kim

CONTENTS

CHAPTER 1

INVISIBLE AMERICANS

In 1962, Michael Harrington published *The Other America*, which awakened America to the extent of poverty in a nation that at the time thought the postwar affluence had solved such problems. Harrington presented persuasive evidence that at least 25 percent of Americans were poor, and it shocked a nation that thought of itself as newly affluent. A middle class was flourishing by the 1960s. Harrington's book and the buoyant economy combined to raise the American people's sense of obligation and commitment to decency. Under President Lyndon Johnson, the country adopted a range of generous programs for the poor, including children, and people of color. This "War on Poverty," though hardly as bold as it could have been, succeeded far more than its later deriders claimed.

But the child poverty rate in America today is 20 to 25 percent as I measure it, and arguably higher, and it has produced no wave of response vaguely similar to Johnson's more than fifty years ago. My purposes here are to document the scourge of child poverty, the many ways it damages children and limits their possibilities, to make clear the immense irresponsibility of the world's richest nation to tolerate basically the highest child poverty rates in the developed world, and to recommend what should be done about it.

There are roughly 13 million officially poor children in America, nearly one in five. If properly measured it would be closer to one in four, and with more honest assumptions more than one in three. In France and Germany only around one in ten children are poor, and by a more stringent test. In the Nordic nations, only one in thirty children are poor. Child poverty is lower in these nations not because the economy produces fewer poor people but because social policies are directed at supporting the poor more generously and efficiently than in the United States.

Our struggling children lack material goods and services, including minimally decent shelter and healthcare. The level of material deprivation, or *hardship*, as analysts call it, is much higher than the government-reported poverty rate. Some analysts argue that child poverty is lower because parents don't remember and don't fully report income from government programs on government surveys. Others note that many people underreport earned income. Even with underreporting, poverty rates would be higher than in almost any other rich nation. Moreover, according to the latest studies, well over one in three American children live in a household with a significant deprivation: inadequate food, lack of access to medical care due to its cost, seriously overcrowded housing, and so on.

These children are well aware of their poverty, and

they live not merely in deprivation but also in shame. They see themselves as irredeemable outsiders. They watch television and observe how others live; they see movie ads even if they can't afford to go to the movies. They flip through sophisticated comic books, which they cannot buy. Debilitating pessimism is thrust upon them at a young age. When middle-class Americans scoff at poor kids because parents buy them the latest expensive sneakers and iPhones, they are unaware that these kids demand these things not to show off but mostly to belong, a deep need of which they are mostly deprived.

I will argue that poor children have many requirements, but above all they need money.

The distress and consequences of child poverty are too often ignored. Reducing child poverty is more consequential than reducing poverty among other groups due to its longer term effects. Overwhelming evidence makes clear that poverty results in lasting damage to poor children compared to middle-income children. Their cognitive abilities are seriously reduced, their emotions are destabilized, and their health is compromised over a wide range of debilities. They often live in physical and emotional pain. Infant mortality is higher in the United States than in other rich nations. Such studies are adjusted for race, ethnicity, and parental education to isolate the effects of low income itself.

Child poverty was hardly mentioned in the 2016 presidential primary battles by Democrats or Republicans, nor in the general election campaign. Some Democratic presidential candidates are only now beginning to formulate policies aimed at incomes below the median—below the halfway point of workers' wages. But these policies, given stagnating incomes for more than a generation, typically don't go far enough.

Such damage has measurable longer-term consequences for the productivy of poor children when they become adults, their health costs, and the costs of crime. A stunning recent analysis finds that GDP is up to $1 trillion lower as a result of child poverty, or more than 5 percent. Many analysts agree this is a reasonable, if as I say shocking, number. It is mostly due to reduced labor productivity of workers, higher health costs, and the costs of crime, including incarceration. Child poverty affects all of us.

The American social policy system of the last forty years emphasizes work for parents through income tax credits, which are not the best way to reduce poverty. Instead, I will advance a position embraced by a burgeoning number of academics: America should be distributing substantial cash grants to all families with children without conditions. Better-off families will have much of the income taxed away.

Why not childhood benefits only to poor families? America's most successful social programs, including Social Security, Medicare, and unemployment insurance, are all universal. The deduction of interest on home mortgages is similarly available to all homeowners. And primary and secondary education is free for all children in America. Such universal programs have persistent and widespread political support. These are what made America great. A universal program will also cover those children considered merely "near-poor" by the current official poverty measures—I will argue that these children are in fact truly poor.

In tracing the causes of America's neglect of poverty through its historical ideology, its longstanding skepticism of the poor, its continuing deep-seated racism and anti-immigrant attitudes, and a superficial scholarship of dependency, I will bring attention to the deliberate official understating of the numbers of the poor. The official poverty measure in America is one of the most irresponsible statistics produced by the government. I will closely examine the damage done to poor children, and describe how these children actually live.

MONEY MATTERS

Poor children and their parents have so many needs, but cash should be the highest priority. Several strands of research over the past twenty years have helped form a consensus among leading academics that cash income spent by parents can reduce disadvantages for children significantly. The research has partly been based on experiments when some poor groups have suddenly had access to more money than others, due, for example, to increases in the generosity of federal social programs. The studies show that those poor children do better in school, are more likely to graduate from high school, are often more stable emotionally, are healthier, make higher wages as adults, avoid incarceration, and live longer. Provocative historical sociology studies on cash relief programs begun more than a hundred years ago have convincingly found longer life spans resulting from greater incomes, as they follow recipients to their death. Enabling families to use cash as they choose without conditions has been a constructive solution in Europe and Canada. Parents spend the money by and large on their kids' needs, and unconditional cash distributions minimize the stigma of poverty, reducing the patronizing attitudes of government officials and society at large.

That America does not provide adequate housing for the poor, decent institutions for childcare, adequate levels of food subsidy, or public education of equal quality is no secret. These needs absorb significant analytical time, institutional attention, and government money, but corrective actions are woefully slow in formulation and fall short of satisfying the need.

Child poverty is too punishing and harmful to wait years for results—especially when cash distributions can help today. A family with two children being provided $300 to $400 for each child when typical decent housing costs roughly $600 or $700 a month can improve their standard of living immediately. The additional income significantly raises the family food and clothing budgets. It may help buy decent childcare for working mothers. Some scholars believe poverty can be cut in half almost immediately for roughly $90 to $110 billion of federal funding a year.

WHY SOCIAL POLICIES ARE INADEQUATE

Since the 1990s, America's new and substantial social programs, including welfare reform and the expanded

Earned Income Tax Credit (EITC), have been mostly designed to get poor parents to work. Their benefits are determined by how much they make. This attitude toward poverty policy reflects a centuries-old battle in America about who the deserving poor are. American leaders have largely concluded that only those who work deserve government aid. Even food stamps have a work requirement. Welfare has changed, but poverty rates have remained high.

Tax credits, which as implied reduce taxes owed, are inefficient and favor the better-off among low-income people rather than very poor Americans. Poverty rates have fallen as a result since the 1990s, but not as much as even some progressive advocates claim, an issue we will address late in the book. Tax credits do not in themselves create either the jobs or the opportunities America badly needs. Studies have found that tax credits also "pushed down somewhat wages in low-skilled labor markets in general. This wage reduction decreases the earnings and employment of others." Direct cash aid is denigrated by both the left and the right as a waste and inducement to laziness and abuse. But the social policies of today are failing. The poorest of the poor are wantonly neglected, including poor children, under the new American social regime. The sheer number of poor children is a moral tragedy and an appalling waste of precious resources.

THE UBIQUITOUS POOR

If you're an American, relentless family poverty is nearby. It's growing in formerly rich suburbs like Nas-

sau and Suffolk Counties in New York. It's now near
the national average in newly rich areas like Santa Clara
County in Silicon Valley (12.3 percent). It remains in
the Deep South and the agricultural Southwest, where
there are the greatest number of poor counties in the
country. It is in the Inland Empire of California and
persists in Appalachia and in Washington, D.C. People
in the citadels of old money, in the elite neighborhoods
of Chicago and New York, know it is only a few blocks
or at most a couple of miles away—if they think about
it at all. Poverty is even more concentrated in recent
years than it was in the 1990s. "There are now more
census tracts of concentrated poverty than have ever
been recorded before," writes the policy scholar Paul
Jargowsky.

A higher proportion of children are poor than
adults. To stick for the moment with the official poverty measure, the child poverty rate is 17.5 percent versus
12.3 percent for adults. An updated alternative poverty
measure developed by the federal government, but also
with flaws, is called the Supplemental Poverty Measure.
I believe it, too, understates child poverty. It places child
poverty at 15.6 percent, but adults' poverty is more than
2 percentage points lower.

Put another way, children comprise roughly one-
quarter of the population but one-third of the official
poor. More than one out of three American children
live in official poverty for at least one year. By European poverty measures, the rate could approach one in
two. More white children are officially poor than white
adults, more black children than black adults, and more

Hispanic children than Hispanic adults. One reason there are more poor children than adults is the high number of single-parent households, often headed by women, whose poverty levels are particularly high, in part because there is only one income. The proportion of single-mother households in Europe is almost as high as it is in America, yet their child poverty rates are far lower as a result of adequate social programs.

While tax credits can help, as have improvements in access to health insurance for children, far more attention is paid to the elderly in America than to children. Aid for the elderly, including Social Security, a cash program, and Medicare, is commendable and necessary. But American social programs raise twice as many elderly out of official poverty than they do poor children. The Agriculture Department's measure of food insecurity is more than twice as high for children as for the elderly, strongly suggesting that children's poverty rates are understated. To put it simply, children do not have enough food to eat.

In an age where better-off parents spend so much more to enrich their children's lives than they once did—one estimate is an additional $10,000 a year in developmental expenses for their children—poor children are falling even further behind. To the extent they don't or can't develop their full potential, the economy is significantly undermined. When poor children do not receive adequate aid, collateral damage is done to their mothers, who often don't have access to jobs, are subject to racial and gender pay gaps, and have inadequate help in a society that now virtually demands that women work and incarcerates poor men, particularly men of color.

MEASURING POVERTY

The irresponsible and cavalier way America calculates how many people are poor reflects its long-standing skepticism about who is poor and its historical lack of sensitivity to poverty. Even well-meaning analysts oversimplify the child poverty problem because they are content to use official measures as true estimates of poverty. Those estimates are inaccurate and biased.

There was no official poverty line in America until 1969, though there were many estimates of the number of poor since the 1800s. The line finally adopted, the Official Poverty Measure (OPM), is among the least sensible and misleading statistics the U.S. government produces. The basis for the OPM has not been updated in more than fifty years. It is a low rate that has not kept up with changing standards of living, a measure that few other nations use. When first adopted, the poverty line was about 50 percent of typical household income (the median). Today, adjusted for inflation, the line is 30 percent of median household income. There is no scientific or rational basis for that discrepancy.

Alternative poverty measures have been devised, notably the Supplemental Poverty Measure (SPM), which has been endorsed by the Census Bureau, the agency that calculates the OPM. The SPM is a more complex, up-to-date, and comprehensive measure, which includes government programs. The OPM includes only cash income. Yet it, too, is inadequate to the problem. As of early 2019, the SPM raised the poverty line only slightly above the OPM, from $24,800 for a family of two adults and two children to roughly $27,000.

The pressure for four to live within an SPM budget of $27,000 is intense. The rent for a very modest two-bedroom apartment in many locations is roughly $800. That leaves about $350 a week, including government programs, for an officially poor family of four for food, childcare (which can be very expensive), clothing, entertainment, schoolbooks, taxes, and the rest. Add a reasonable estimate to run a car at $1,000 a month, but not likely less than $500, and money for absolute necessities cited above is down to less than a couple of hundred dollars a week. Doing without a car in most of America is a serious handicap. Public transportation for two workers could easily run $300 a month. The United Way Alice Project finds that 43 percent of American households, nearly 51 million, can't afford to meet the costs cited above plus a smartphone. A national survey done by Gallup every few years finds that people think a family of four must earn roughly $50,000 a year just to "get along." If the poverty line were moderately realistic, official poverty rates would be significantly higher, and the nation, even its legislators, would be more aware and perhaps more sensitive to the tragedy unfolding. Many believe that an informal definition of low income in America is twice the official poverty line, or about that same $50,000 a year for a family of four. At twice the current poverty line, more than 40 percent of children live in low-income families in America, or more than 30 million children.

The OPM should conservatively be $37,000 dollars a year for a family of four, about 50 percent higher than it currently is. This would leave it close to the 50 percent level of median household income it was in 1969. Such a level would add another 8 or so million to the number of poor children in America.

My own ideal definition of a useful poverty measure would be this: the level below which we know that short- and long-term damage is being done to children. There are examples of such poverty lines drawn before World War II and even in the 1800s. Such an idea is not now a formal consideration in academic circles, partly because choosing such a threshold for damage would be difficult given the state of the research. Future research into damage done, however, may make it easier to do. Measuring it this way would reinforce the reasonableness of a poverty line at 1.5 times the current OPM or higher.

So far, I have been referring to families who live near the poverty line. But nearly 6 million children live in families that earn half or less of the official poverty line, which policy experts call deep poverty. Nearly 20 million of all Americans live in deep poverty today. For a family of four, this is roughly $12,500 a year, or a little more than $1,000 a month, not nearly enough for both minimal nutrition and housing. This is squalor. These especially low-income children suffer measurably worse harm. There are 3 million children who live, before counting food stamps, on $2 a day in cash, the poverty rate devised by the World Bank for poor and developing nations. This is informally known as extreme poverty, though the terms *deep* and *extreme* are sometimes used interchangeably. Counting food stamps would reduce this estimate, but food stamps are not the equivalent of cash.

For those in the bottom half of the poverty population, welfare is profoundly inadequate, in good part a result of the reforms of the 1990s under Bill Clinton. If a family earns no or little income, which has been increasingly likely in the last thirty years of declining pay and few good jobs, America is severely punishing them. The only major cash or quasi-cash welfare programs are food stamps, now known as the Supplemental Nutrition Assistance Program (SNAP), and Temporary Assistance to Needy Families (TANF), the Clinton welfare reform program of 1996, which is far less generous than the welfare system it replaced. If a family with children is lucky enough to receive both programs (many states resist allowing families onto TANF), the income from these programs will on average amount to only 55 percent of the already low official poverty measure. In seventeen states the total is under 50 percent of the OPM; in one state, Mississippi, less than 40 percent of the official poverty line.

DESERVINGNESS

America has long been resistant to adequate poverty policies because of its strong strain of thinking that the poor are responsible for their own situation, no matter their suffering. On balance, economists have not helped enough, and many have made matters far worse. The inherent bias among even the best of them is usually that economic growth will "cure" poverty, but that has never been the case. Economic growth has reduced extreme poverty, notably in some of today's developing nations with improved social policies, but nowhere has it nearly eliminated it. In America, inadequate opportunities, belief in small government, institutional prejudices among banks and real estate developers, racial bias in education and labor markets, underfunded schools, and a desire by many powerful businesses for poor workers who won't demand higher wages all contribute to the persistence of large numbers of poor who suffer and lead minimized lives. History has shown unambiguously that government assistance is necessary to alleviate this suffering.

There are many factors that can worsen the damaging consequences of poverty, including a dearth of affordable housing, crime-ridden neighborhoods, poor schools, and inadequate child services. Many experts insist we should fix most of them. A study just released in 2019 under the auspices of the National Academy of Sciences proposed four different plans to reduce child poverty, for example. The authors included tax credits and work requirements in each of their plans, along with other proposals, including cash allowances. Their mandate was to propose policies that reduce child poverty. Advocates of such a full-court press against child poverty, however, may distract from getting the job done.

For policymakers, there is a more optimistic and more direct answer. The finding that money alone can make a large difference amounts to a major breakthrough. "One of the odd aspects of the history of writing about poverty," writes the historian Michael Katz, "is the avoidance of the simple view that people are poor because they lack money. Again, a cynical historian could see much of the writing on poverty as an elaborate dance choreographed to stay away from the point."

REFORMS

In Europe, poverty is considered a "relative" condition compared to the rest of society, usually 50 to 60 percent of the median family's income—the family whose income is in the middle of the pack. As society gets richer overall, the poverty measure will rise. Adopting that measure in America would provide a metric, if an imperfect one, of social inclusion—giving the poor the opportunity to live a full civic and economic life as economies prosper and material needs change.

We should abide by two principles in fashioning an income support program: universality—a cash program for all children, not just the poor—and nonpaternalism, meaning that recipients decide how to use their cash distribution as they see fit. My direct proposal is to establish an unconditional monthly cash allowance for all children in America of $4,000 to $5,000 a year. As I said, it will be taxable, so wealthy families will have the benefits largely taxed away.

THE NEOLIBERAL CONVERSION

The neoliberal conversion of America that began in the 1970s and hardened in the 1980s became more extreme under President Donald Trump. A government of more tax reductions and promises of deep cuts in social spending cannot easily be withstood by a nation that has already lived with a generation of inadequate policies. Child poverty is bound to worsen. Under similar policies in England, during the regime of Margaret Thatcher, child poverty soared. After reforms under the Labour government, which reduced poverty, it rose again in recent years when Conservatives cut social spending. The Trump administration has scandalously claimed based on duplicitous use of data that general poverty is only 3 percent in America, rather than the official estimates of 12 to 13 percent (and realistic estimates that it is much higher). Child poverty was minimal in their calculations as they shamelessly manipulated the data. The conservative economists whose research the claims were based on themselves conceded they were not seeking a specific poverty rate. The rate of 3 percent was arbitrary. It could also have been as high as 12.7 percent under slightly different assumptions.

In a time when we avidly discuss and worry about the future of the nation's productivity and prospects for growth, it is hard to believe that we are willing to discard 20 to 25 percent or more of the population by not providing them an adequate standard of living early in their lives, depriving them of the foundation necessary to become productive workers. As noted a reasonable

cost to us all is $1 trillion in lost national income—
reduced GDP.

Poverty is one of the main battlefields of American
ideology. Warring camps have been fighting over it for a
couple of centuries. At one end of the spectrum are the
individualists, who believe poverty is mostly the result
of individual failings, and at the other end are those
who see the cause in structural social and economic ele-
ments including prejudice, scarce jobs, and low wages.

The individualists have usually won out in America, prevailing again since the 1980s and 1990s. Poverty, Michael Katz has written, has been a third rail to
policymakers, including Democrats, for more than a
generation. This misguided course can be righted.

CHAPTER 2

HOW POOR CHILDREN LIVE

It's important to see the conditions in which poor children live, and the stories of children in poverty must begin with hunger.

THE MODERN FOOD TRAGEDY

Not long ago, a group of poverty skeptics argued that hunger's presence in America was exaggerated. The legal scholar and Reagan adviser Edwin Meese III claimed in 1983 he'd never seen "any authoritative figures that there are hungry children" in America. Some people, Meese said, go to soup kitchens "because the food is free and . . . that's easier than paying for it." Similar charges are made today. But no one can contest that there are measurable consequences of taking in an inadequate amount of good food.

The U.S. Agriculture Department and the Census Department survey households annually to determine their access to adequate food. The federal government has developed two categories of food security to determine the adequacy of financial budgets. "Low food security" involves regularly buying cheaper, less nutritious, filler foods due to limited budgets. "Very low food security" involves missing meals regularly and is seen as a measure of outright persistent hunger.

Children who live in families with low food security are more likely to be both obese and diabetic. Poor prenatal nutrition is statistically related to low birth weight and stunted children. Low food security is also related to a range of adverse consequences, including slow cognitive development, a greater likelihood of hospital visits, and decreases in school performance.

Some 44 percent of those identified as poor children have low food security. The number typically spikes during economic recessions when poverty rates rise. Food insecurity rose significantly during the Great Recession—notably in 2008 and 2009—but fell as the economy "recovered."

In fact, government surveys found that food insecurity is higher than average for families with income up to 200 percent of the poverty line. There is no scarcity of hunger in America today.

Hunger is the first and most persistent experience of poverty for children in America. There was severe starvation and indeed death in America, notably in the Deep South, as recently as the late 1960s. The War on Poverty and Great Society programs at last reduced that risk by the 1970s. But to this day the everyday lives of poor children are built around the availability of food—

that is the primary way they learn they are different and sense they are inferior. It is how they are initially introduced to being poor, how they become conscious of poverty, and how they become ashamed of it.

Jesús de los Santos was born in the mid-1980s into poverty in Edinburg, Texas, in Hidalgo County, along the Mexican border. He now has a master's degree in sociology from the University of Michigan, but it was a long, very difficult, and uncertain path.

His mother, Nancy Lopez, was born in America of Mexican immigrants and was a farmworker all her life. Jesús had two brothers and a sister; his father, a trucker, had been jailed (probably, de los Santos vaguely remembers, because he took part in a drug-selling operation to make more money) and later left the family. The family received cash welfare payments under the Aid to Families with Dependent Children program, which had been expanded by Lyndon Johnson. They also received food stamps. These were not nearly enough to raise the family's income above the poverty line.

They all lived in a trailer, sleeping together in one room, and they siphoned electricity through an extension cord attached to a power line. Their windows were repeatedly broken by thieves who stole their food and modest valuables. Eventually they left the door open.

At the beginning of the month, when the food stamps arrived, his mother stocked up on staples like rice and beans. That began a different kind of battle, this one with rats, cockroaches, and ants. She made them pancakes almost every day to fill their bellies. He distinctly remembers his hunger and how he and his siblings complained daily: Jesús says the food stamps always ran out before the end of the month.

As a child he felt shame that his family had to use food stamps and get their meals from the free pantries nearby—though he recalled how eagerly they took the fresh chicken, beef, vegetables, and fruit when available. He looked forward to and came to depend on free school lunches once he reached school age, a federal program. His mother bought their clothing at deep discount stores. His mother did not, or could not, take him to doctors or dentists, though he complained of pain as a child. His mouth still hurts. He went to primary school with many children who were better off and better dressed than he.

Luckily, Jesús was a gifted student, and primary school administrators almost immediately placed him in classes for advanced children. He was good at school, he says, in part because his mother was a constant reader, mostly of romance novels. Reading was contagious. "You could entertain yourself by cracking a book," he says. "I'd read everything I could get from the library. Our video recorders and TVs were constantly stolen, so we stopped buying them."

His reading background, however, did not protect him from the risks of the neighborhood. Even in primary school he fell in with the "bad" kids. By junior high school he was taking drugs and involved with gangs.

He says all his siblings were emotionally troubled, himself included. He experienced bouts of depression and uncontrollable rage. Some of his friends were arrested, and he says he was lucky to escape the juvenile offender system. For all his ability, studying was not his priority, and his grades were poor. By high school, his mother sent him to a middle-class suburb in Ohio to live with an uncle. He still did not apply himself, but he graduated nonetheless.

After a few years working as a cook, and a bout of homelessness, he applied and was accepted to Texas Community College. Now that he was older and more experienced, his motivation was high and he studied hard. He earned A's and was accepted on scholarship to graduate school at the University of Michigan. He was a superb student, according to his adviser. Still, it took him quite a while, perhaps because of bias against Hispanics, to land his current job as a learning and development facilitator in Austin, Texas.

This is not a story about the American dream. Jesús does not feel he is yet a secure middle-class American. Despite his considerable innate talent and hard work, a middle-class life is far from assured. One senses a persistent insecurity in him. Perhaps it is a fear that he will be very poor again.

Progress has been made in reducing the hardship of poverty as a result of new or expanded federal programs, some of which are supplemented by state programs. Medicaid (medical insurance for the poor) was made available to all low-income children in the 1980s, not just to those in families receiving welfare. If you worked and earned enough, the Earned Income Tax Credit (EITC) was now widely available, and had been made more generous in the 1990s. The Child Tax Credit (CTC) was established in 1997. CHIP, the child health insurance program sponsored by Senators Ted Kennedy and Orrin Hatch (a noteworthy bipartisan achievement), had improved healthcare for many since its adoption in 1997. It provides health insurance to children in families that earn a bit too much to qualify for Medicaid.

But while many have been helped, and the child poverty rate has fallen, it is still both too high and undercounted in official governmental measures. Policies based on these measures do not sufficiently reach poor Americans. Most programs, especially those tied to employment, like the EITC, have aided people who earned near or a little above the poverty line, but have not sufficiently aided those further down or in deep poverty (defined as 50 percent of the poverty line). Traditional cash welfare payments under AFDC were restricted in 1996–97, with the adoption of TANF. The health of poor children remains worse than those who are not poor and ranks near the bottom among wealthy nations. Happily, child mortality has fallen over the last two decades, but it has also done so in almost all rich nations.

SNAP, or the Supplemental Nutrition Assistance Program (formerly called food stamps), was designed to supplement the needs of the poor. Started in the late 1930s, it is now a $78-billion-a-year program, and since the controversial welfare reform of 1996 it has become America's principal antipoverty program for many people, especially the very poor. It has been moderately successful, though there are now some work requirements to qualify. Benefits have been raised—and more than 90 percent of these benefits go to those below the poverty line. An exception, fifty-seven percent of the benefits go to those who earn less than half of the poverty line. Research shows that children in families that participate in SNAP have improved cognitive, educational, and health outcomes.

The program's benefits are calculated to fill the gap between what families can afford and their needs as determined by the stingy "Thrifty Budget" of the Agriculture Department. SNAP raised 8.4 million people out of poverty as measured by the SPM in a 2015 survey, 3.8 million of whom were children. Some 2 million children were raised above half the official poverty line (OPM).

Few analysts, though, think SNAP is sufficient. The average benefit in 2019 is $465 a month for a family of four. It now disburses benefits on an electronic card. The average individual benefit is about $125 per person monthly, or about $1.50 a meal.

SNAP is a constant source of political criticism by conservatives who claim abuse is rampant. The evidence of this is minimal. A United Nations examination of poverty in America found little evidence of fraud. Ronald Reagan reduced food benefits, but they were raised in the 1990s and again under President Obama.

Coping practices and food strategies of the poor in the face of food insecurity are deeply influenced by these new programs. Typically, families use all their meager SNAP allowance by the third week of the month—and then a scramble for food begins, which according to surveys, usually involves low-nutrition, high-carbohydrate food like Jesús's pancakes, or chips and sugary break-fast cereals. "The foods that they can afford to buy are high calorie, but low nutrition," noted one worker at an emergency food provider. "They fill the stomach, but they serve to exacerbate the chronic conditions that they face. So the conditions get worse, the people go to the doctor, and their doctors prescribe medicines to combat the chronic conditions. Those medicines cost money, meaning that the households have even less to spend on food, and place those household heads in the same position of trying to decide which necessities they can cut back on or go without. It is a vicious, crazy cycle." Often families skip meals altogether. Bouts of hunger arrive monthly or even more often.

The free or low-cost lunch program for children whose families live on up to 185 percent of the poverty line is another invaluable federal benefit. There is also a similar breakfast program. The lunch program had its origins in piecemeal local policies won by Progressive reformers in the late nineteenth and early twentieth centuries, inspired by Parisian, Swiss, Dutch, Norwe-gian, and English measures to provide meals to school-children. The American program, of course, was widely expanded in the succeeding decades. The lack of lunch and breakfast programs during the summer recess places additional hardship on poor families, though there is now a federal program to supplement food issuance in summer as well.

Move forward thirty years from the time when Jesús de los Santos lived in poverty to another town in the same

Texas county, Hidalgo, where Blanca lived. In a notable series in *The Washington Post*, she told a reporter how she managed the monthly food budget—$460 a month of SNAP benefits—for herself and her two children. By the end of the month, the refrigerator was usually bare and the task of getting the kids to eat nutritionally became nearly impossible. Her fifteen-year-old daughter, Clarissa, had developed tell-tale signs of early-onset diabetes, such as a black circle on her neck from too much insulin creation. Her nine-year-old son, Antonio, was already on cholesterol medication. The school nurse insisted Blanca make an appointment for her children.

The doctor confirmed Clarissa had dangerously high levels of sugar, and Antonio had persistently high levels of cholesterol. He insisted that Clarissa cut her sugar intake, including foods high in carbohydrates. Antonio was ordered to continue his anti-cholesterol medication. "Does that mean I can't eat Cheetos?" Antonio asked. "Yes," the doctor answered.

"One bag a week?"

"No."

Blanca tried to feed her kids well, but the kids resisted. She prepared broccoli one night but they wouldn't eat it unless it was awash in butter; even mole sauce didn't work without a heap of tortilla chips. That night Antonio went to the fridge for his snack. His mother wanted him to make the right choice himself: a piece of fresh fruit, perhaps. But instead he took Super Mario fruit snacks and a Diet Coke to show his dedication to losing weight. For parents, poor kids are just as hard to manage as middle-class kids, but with far fewer healthful food choices.

In another family in Hidalgo, a mother of four, even with a full-time job, had difficulty feeding her children in the summers without the free lunch program in school. In summertime, dinner could include chips, Doritos, bread, leftover doughnuts, Airheads candy, and Dr. Pepper—cheap filler foods.

Come morning, this family waited for the daily summer bus visit with one full meal's worth of food for each child, financed by a federal school vacation program. One of her daughters stood at the window of their home. The bus driver, who knew them well by now, said he had pears, turkey, and biscuits—and asked her whether she was hungry. "Always," she said.

Yolanda Minor, once a home visitor and now a leader of the field staff at Save the Children, says one of the key missions of such visitors is to teach mothers how to sign up for SNAP, visit the food banks and charitable organizations without shame, and determine which foods are truly nutritious. Another is to be sure that pregnant women eat adequately.

A large research literature shows that hunger or poor nutrition for pregnant women has significant destructive impact on their children, including in the long run. Minor has little use for those who claim poor children are eating adequately. "Just watch how fast they eat the food off their plates in school," Yolanda told me.

A long line of poverty analysts in America going back to the late nineteenth century have demanded more discipline of poor mothers when they have drawn up what they considered adequate budgets for poor families. A poor mother living in Baltimore, who has a full-time night job but raises three children, told me how hard it is when the kids are asking for treats in the aisles of the supermarket when you can't afford even the essentials. One poverty expert, after interviewing more than forty poor or near-poor mothers, says that some teach their children not to ask them for a dollar in front of people because it hurts too much when they can't give it to them.

EPISODIC AND PERIODIC POVERTY

The scholars Kathryn Edin and H. Luke Shaefer tell the story of an entrepreneurial white man in Cleveland named Paul who got a middle-income job in a steel mill as a young man, something the younger poor can no longer do. He put himself through college partly by selling his blood plasma, became a medical equipment expert, then built up a pizza business based on money borrowed on his home. The venture thrived enough for him to have three profitable pizza stores.

The financial crisis of 2007 and 2008 clobbered Paul and hundreds of thousands of people like him— white, black, Latino, and Asian—who thought they had secured a near-middle-class life and a future for their children. Paul's pizza businesses failed. The price of his house plummeted, and he almost lost it. "I'm stuck with a $65,000 mortgage on a $15,000 house," as he put it.

His kids and their spouses also lost jobs. They moved in with him, bringing Paul's grandchildren with them; his home became a haven "to twenty extended family members in addition to Paul and Sarah, his wife of forty years." SNAP is now critical to him and his family. He tried to get more SNAP to cover his children and their families, but was unsuccessful.

Consider the plight of Paul's grandchildren. "The front room serves as a bedroom for four of the kids," as Edin and Shaefer tell it. "The finished portion of the basement houses Sam and his six kids. Five more children and Paul's younger daughter are stuffed into a tiny bedroom on the second floor (doubled up in two bunk beds and a single bed). Paul's older daughter and her family are stashed in the tiny attic." With the nation's adoption of TANF, there was virtually no cash welfare to help Paul. His kids now knew abject poverty.

The return of this kind of episodic and periodic poverty is relatively new in the post–World War II period. Based on surveys, incomes have become much more volatile. One survey found that 95 percent of those who earn between 100 and 150 percent of the poverty line fall under the poverty line for at least one month of the year. The source of the volatility is not only lost jobs but also "swings in income within a given job"— another precarious new reality.

When she was a home visitor, Yolanda Minor regularly met with a family in Glosters, a very poor, small community, mostly of trailers, in the Mississippi Delta. I've changed the details of their lives slightly at Yolanda's request. The mother, thirty-four—call her Carol—had a child at sixteen and another not long afterward. Her daughter, now eighteen—call her Marilynne—herself had a baby at sixteen and another a year later. Mother, daughter, and their children now share a mobile home. Yolanda said the cramped quarters created constant stress and tension. One of Yolanda's priorities is to introduce books into their lives. But the kids have no place to read or do their homework.

People often chide women like Carol and Marilynne for having out-of-wedlock children, or for having children as teenagers. Just shape up, they essentially say.

Teenage births are sharply down among all young people—whites, blacks, and Latinos—in part due to the availability of contraception. Meanwhile, pregnancy among unmarried women rose sharply for all groups from 1960 to 2009. (The percentage of all births to unmarried women peaked in 2009 at 41 percent; in 2017, the last year for which we have numbers, it was 39.8 percent.) So while fewer teenagers are having children, more women of all kinds are having children without a husband. These are major social changes, and they have occurred in many nations. While teenage births have dramatically fallen, they do occur—and poor, young mothers and their families scrape together a way to live.

Yolanda, as she did with all her clients, made sure Carol and Marilynne were properly signed up for SNAP and knew how to access the free pantries and food banks in the region. Both Carol and Marilynne worked odd jobs at local stores or did laundry for neighbors. Yolanda wouldn't say if they occasionally sold part of their SNAP for cash, a common though illegal practice among the very poor to pay for electricity or clothing. There is a saying in poor communities: "Heat or eat."

Neither Carol nor Marilynne bothered with TANF because it paid so little and required them to spend too much time qualifying by looking for a job, which they rarely found. SNAP was their only regular income.

HOUSING

Poor children live in significantly worse housing conditions than those with more income. One study found that 85 percent of the homes of poor asthmatic children in cities had detectable cockroach allergen levels. A far higher proportion of minorities than of whites live in such conditions.

Since the mid-1970s, housing has become less affordable for low-income families. "The cost-burdened share of renters doubled from 23.8 percent in the 1960s to 47.5 percent in 2016," concludes a recent Harvard study, "as housing costs and household incomes steadily diverged." Today, 83 percent of renters with incomes under $15,000 are housing-cost-burdened (paying rents more than 30 percent of their income), as are 77 percent of those with incomes between $15,000 and $29,999. One study found that families paying 50 percent or more of their income in rent or housing costs—a level labeled "severely rent burdened"—had an average of $565 left a month for all other expenses. A higher proportion of blacks and Latinos fall into this category. The pattern holds whether poor families are renters or homeowners. "A similar proportion of low-income homeowners and renters are severely cost burdened," a 2017 study found. "Homeowners are just as vulnerable to severe housing cost burdens as renters at the same income level." The scholar Matthew Desmond writes, "The majority of poor renting families in America now devote at least half of their income to covering housing costs."

Too often the poor are relegated to the worst quality of housing, in high-poverty neighborhoods that are often crime-ridden and where drugs are common and toxins are high, and where there are few public facilities like parks and libraries. They also must live in overcrowded quarters, which studies show is one of the most damaging conditions for children.

Poor children move far more often than do the non-poor, and evidence shows that frequent moving is damaging. Housing instability damages educational performance and health, affects children's ability to focus, and, of course, reduces days in school. Evidence shows that housing subsidies, in turn, improve child outcomes when families move to more affordable and better quarters.

It would be hard to find a reasonable analyst who believes that government subsidies for housing are adequate. Senator Elizabeth Warren introduced a bill to expand funds sharply for the building of affordable housing. Other Democrats with presidential aspirations proposed new housing subsidies as well. Tenants would also benefit from more access to legal counsel when threatened with eviction, and emergency aid for sudden losses of income.

Exposure to lead hazards is also far more common for poor children than those from non-poor families. At least half a million and as many as 1.2 million children under six have elevated levels of lead in their blood.

EVICTIONS

Matthew Desmond points out that there is an estimable tradition of housing studies of the poor beginning with such classics as Friedrich Engels's 1844 *The Condition of the Working Class in England* and Jacob Riis's *How the Other Half Lives*. Sociological analysis of housing has in recent decades been neglected, he points out, in favor of research on government housing policy.

But, as Desmond shows, legal evictions of the poor are rising rapidly. In his book *Evicted: Poverty and Profit in the American City*, Desmond investigates court records to determine the causes and frequency of eviction. Living for six months in a poor neighborhood in Milwaukee, he interviewed many of those evicted in housing court. He finds that about one in twenty-five renters are evicted each year in Milwaukee. In subsequent work he has found cities with twice, even four times, that rate. African American women are hardest hit, with one in five, by his estimate, evicted each year.

If you go to eviction court, you will see many children. It's mostly mothers and children, Desmond writes: "The sound of eviction court was a soft hum of dozens of people sighing, coughing, murmuring, and whispering to children interspersed with the cadence of a name, a pause, and three loud thumps of the stamp." Housing courts in New York City even have daycare units (in the Bronx, Queens, and Manhattan—but not in Brooklyn, where eviction and gentrification are notoriously widespread). Evictions usually occur for lack of payment, but there are many potential violations landlords can use to rid themselves of an unwanted tenant. Desmond and his researchers believe that 2.3 million people received an eviction notice in America in 2016. That's twice the number arrested for drug possession.

Rising rents are the main cause of increasing evictions, particularly of women—along with stagnating or falling wages for the jobs working-class women typically hold. Eviction is to black women what incarceration is to men, Desmond writes.

An eviction notice will make it hard to get another lease and also hard to qualify for public housing. Eviction often leads to homelessness.

HOMELESSNESS AND SHELTERS

The homeless crisis in America accelerated under Ronald Reagan, and it continues unabated today. Thirty-three percent of homeless people today are families with children, and extreme poverty is the best predictor of family homelessness. Recent studies estimate that 2.5 million children will be homeless in America some part of this year, most of whom live with families in shelters or on an ad-hoc and temporary basis with friends and family. Some live alone in these shelters. Often they must move, even nightly. Others move from apartment to apartment with a parent, or to hotels. Some one in seven children in New York City public primary schools will be homeless at some point during their elementary education if the crisis continues. In the 2015–16 school year alone, roughly 100,000 New York City schoolchildren were homeless; of these, 33,000 lived in shelters.

The federal government reports that homeless children are twice as likely to experience hunger as their non-homeless peers.

One out of three homeless children are separated from their families. Evidence is abundant that homeless children pay a price in poor health, cognitive delay, and low graduation rates.

Lauren is a therapist at a Lower East Side grade school in Manhattan. She deals in particular with abused or extremely disadvantaged children. Many of the children she aids live in shelters. Mark, whose name is changed, is one of the students she worries most about. His mother is likely an alcoholic, she says. Child Services had taken him away from her repeatedly for neglect. When Mark is living with his mother, he has no permanent residence, staying with her at a shelter or with her friends. She is often not home at night.

"Every day is a different day with Mark," Lauren says. "He is often extremely hungry, tired, noticeably lethargic, moody." He is doing poorly in school, and he is well aware of it. He is eleven but is only in third grade, having been left back twice.

Brianna is now a well-paid social worker, but she and her husband went through bouts of homelessness. For a while, they and their two children lived in a motel, then in a shelter. Sleeping arrangements in these programs are often segregated by sex, and families are frequently broken up in homeless shelters. Brianna's shelter did not allow her to bring medications there for her younger boy with severe asthma. The boy had to be sent to a motel with her husband.

White communities in Appalachia, particularly Kentucky and Tennessee, have among the highest child poverty rates in America, sometimes almost 50 percent. In Lake County, Tennessee, 46 percent of children live in poverty; in Hancock County, 42 percent. Shelters in these communities, like so many in America, are highly uneven in quality and impose greatly on the lives of their residents.

Edin and Shaefer, writing of shelters even in large cities with relatively advanced social programs, say, "Some take only women with children under age five. Others require attendance at religious services. Some require that you have recently lost a home, while others mandate a criminal background check. Some have terrific websites, while others are riddled with out-of-date information. Some you can only call, and others you find out about only through word of mouth. Thus, the search for a place to stay can take days of work. And let's say that you finally find a place for which you are eligible and that happens to have room. To get to your new accommodations, you might find yourself traipsing across the city with all your worldly possessions, which is hard to do when you have no money."

PUBLIC CHILDCARE

America has been transformed in the last generation into a nation where mothers almost universally work.

Yet there is no federal paid leave program for new mothers in America, unlike in many other nations. Neither is there widely available free, high-quality public childcare in the United States.

TANF provided funds for childcare services in tandem with work requirements for welfare recipients, but the increase in funding was small. The federal government has not made the contemporary age of personal responsibility easy for the newly working poor mother, explains the public policy scholar Ajay Chaudry. Indeed, little attention was originally paid to the impact on children in the studies supporting the adoption of TANF in the 1990s. Rarely did the businesses where the low-income mothers, often TANF recipients, worked provide decent childcare services. More federal funds were made available by the 2018 Congress, but Chaudry and others argue there is a long way to go.

The children typically can't speak of their deprivation, but the mothers do. Free high-quality childcare is tragically scarce. Meanwhile, research now unambiguously shows that the early years of childhood are the most formative.

Part of the solution is emerging in New York City, with its popular new universal pre-kindergarten program for four-year-olds (and a program for three-year-olds in early implementation). But even here, parents of poor children still find it difficult to access childcare. A confusing patchwork of programs and types of childcare centers are grouped under the banner "universal pre-K": nursery programs, including the federal Head Start and Early Head Start programs, formal daycare centers in the private sector, and public school pre-K. Each has its own intake methods and rules. Partially, this is a result of the de Blasio administration's policy design in knitting together the already existing welter of city, state, and federally funded childcare services. But this uneven and combined childcare policy is also rooted in immigrant and ethnic groups' demand for care and instruction in their own languages, communities, and neighborhoods.

A universal public sector childcare option at the federal level would serve to buttress, complement, and unify this patchwork of free pre-K providers, establishing benchmarks and a model for quality, ease of enrollment, non-discrimination, and curriculum, beyond the regulations. Several presidential condidates are now proposing such programs. But my view is that we can't wait for such legislation; more money to poor mothers would help now.

HEALTH

Despite impressive advances in the availability of health insurance, including Obamacare, poor children still do not receive sufficient preventive and emergency care. Poor nutrition is a direct cause, of course, of poor health. In surveys, parents of children in poverty regularly rate their children's health as fair or poor.

American women in poverty, as noted, are far more likely to deliver low-birth-weight babies than non-poor women; one study put the likelihood of poor mothers giving birth to a low-birth-weight child at 2.37 times the rate of women whose incomes were in the top 20 percent of households. The low-birth-weight rate for black mothers is roughly twice what it is for whites. In international comparisons, there is a significantly higher incidence of low-birth-weight and stunted babies in America than in most of Europe.

Chris Rogers's story was closely followed by the Children's Defense Fund. He was born in 2000 to Ana Rogers, then nineteen, and soon developed a serious earache. Ana was a single working mother of Hispanic descent who had moved from Texas to Cincinnati. We know little about Chris's father, who was himself the son of an African American auto parts worker who'd lost his job when his company moved south, leaving his family to find work elsewhere.

Doses of aspirin prescribed by doctors did not subdue newborn Chris's pain. He was then prescribed with an antibiotic, the conventional prescription for ear infections. Chris would need further medical attention, which he got months later. Middle-class kids would not have had to wait as long. Tubes ran from Chris's ear to drain the damaging fluids.

Critics often, even typically, blame a child's troubles on the irresponsibility of parents, but there is no indication that Ana was anything but a devoted parent. Later, President Obama's Affordable Care Act relieved some of this burden in the states that adopted Medicaid. But the percentage of those who received Medicaid ben-

efits has been uneven, partly due to obstacles created by
right-wing state governments.

America *has* nevertheless sharply raised the number
of children who are covered by government-paid health
insurance. Some 95 percent of children now have insurance for at least part of the year. There were extensions
of Medicaid in the 1980s and 1990s, and in thirty-seven
states under Obama's Affordable Care Act. CHIP,
which provides insurance for poor children whose
families have incomes too high to qualify for Medicaid,
added more children to coverage since its inception in
1997.

The benefits of these programs to children's mortality and birth weight have been well documented,
though they remain significantly worse than in other
rich nations. A key challenge, though, is getting parents to sign up. Schools are integral to this process,
and they use special Medicaid funding to support their
efforts and maintain health personnel on the premises.
Yet there are gaps in coverage, especially in rural areas.
Republicans' efforts to cut Medicaid and add work benefits for recipients whose income is too high to qualify
for Medicaid seriously jeopardize a system that is only
now becoming adequate.

After being treated for his ear infection, Chris started
to talk when he was two, later than the average child,
but his speech was slurred. Over time he remained well
behind in learning the alphabet—he knew only a few
letters—and his vocabulary was below average for his

age. Without Chris's grandmother to serve as babysitter and provide moral support, Ana and Chris might have wound up in one of Cincinnati's crowded shelters.

As Chris grew older, he was increasingly frustrated. Once in kindergarten, Chris became especially violent, even dangerous. He hit and bit his classmates, looked under girls' dresses, gave teachers and, once, the principal the middle finger. Yet sometimes he spontaneously started to cry in his classroom. His grandmother says he would often arrive at school at eight and she would get a call by nine to take him home.

When Chris tackled his kindergarten teacher, throwing him to the ground, he was expelled from his school, Hayes Elementary in Cincinnati's West End. Subsequently, the *Cincinnati Enquirer* did a special report on the city's troubled public schools. Chris was featured on the front page.

His grandmother says the article turned out to be the break of his young life. He got access to treatments unavailable to most of the kids where he grew up. A teacher qualified him for special education classes at another school. He was also referred to the Developmental Disorders Department at Children's Hospital. There a psychiatrist diagnosed his attention deficit disorder and put him on medication.

Finally, he was accepted to a special class at a children's home for those with behavioral and emotional problems, which otherwise had a long waiting list. The school district at the time spent $20,000 a year on each of these children, compared to $11,000 per child in public school. Chris became mainstreamed and now leads a life closer to normal given his disabilities, the life of a middle-class child.

"School is the only organization where a relationship between meaningful people and children can take place on an ongoing basis and compensate for the difficult conditions that interfered with the growth of many," said an Ohio child psychologist. "Those kids who haven't had the socializing and learning experiences that middle-class kids often have are treated as dumb, bad, or unable to handle themselves."

We don't know how much psychological stress or physical pain Chris suffered as an infant and young child, but we can make an educated guess. If you went to Cincinnati fifteen years ago, you'd have seen a city being partly revitalized after its fall from prosperity during the de-industrialization of America's Rust Belt beginning in the 1970s. Its rate of child poverty is now more than 46 percent—in other words, nearly half of children in this once booming city. The rate is higher for children under five.

In Chris's neighborhood, all the schools were on academic watch. They were also especially strict— Cincinnati schools instituted a zero tolerance policy in the early 1990s, which reflected the national set of new anti-crime policies, such as mandatory sentencing, then being implemented as part of the federal War on Drugs and inner-city crime. In some cases, principals by regulation had no alternative but to suspend Chris.

Funding for these schools was on average one-third of what it was in better-off neighborhoods in Ohio. The level was inadequate for treating difficult children.

Some 70 percent of children in Cincinnati's public schools were black, and the teachers and administrators were overwhelmingly white. Ana rejoiced when she found one school with a handful of black teachers.

THE GEOGRAPHY OF POVERTY

By density, America's West and South remain the poorest regions in the nation, despite the general focus on and public image of urban poverty in the Northeast and industrial Midwest.

Conditions for the poor in most high-poverty inner-city neighborhoods are grueling. Schools are bad, dropout rates are high, jobs are few in number, social services are scant, and crime is often more serious than elsewhere. Many scholars have argued that concentration promotes the intergenerational passage of poverty that is so often attributed to a "culture of poverty."

This concentration of poverty briefly declined in the 1990s as the poverty rate fell during the economic boom. The political scientist Paul Jargowsky, a veteran investigator of the concentration of poverty, recently updated Census Bureau data. He found that poverty concentration started to rise rapidly again in the late 1990s and now is at historically high levels. In other words, America is returning to the extreme ghettoization of poverty. These enclaves and barrios, he argues, were "not the value-free outcome of the impartial workings of the housing market. Rather, in large measure, they are the inevitable and predictable consequences of deliberate policy choices." In particular, he emphasizes the impact of inadequate affordable housing outside and increasingly inside the central cities. The Clinton-era programs that demolished public housing and dispersed the urban poor under the banner of reducing the concentration of poverty failed. They merely shifted the geography of poverty.

The number of those who live in high-poverty enclaves, defined as areas in which the poverty rate is 40 percent or more, has doubled since the late 1990s, according to Jargowsky. The most rapid growth in concentration has been in the Midwest, the Middle Atlantic states, the Southwest, and the state of Mississippi. As the sociologist William Julius Wilson and others have long argued, such segregated and poor neighborhoods severely compound the disadvantages of poverty.

This trend places an added burden on children of color. A higher percentage of both black and Latino children live in high-poverty neighborhoods than do black or Latino adults. The concentration of the black poor has been most intense. One in four blacks and one in six Hispanics now live in high-poverty neighborhoods. Only one in thirteen whites do so. A high proportion of blacks also live in near-poverty areas. As a result, a high proportion of their children also live in neighborhoods that are poor. Thus, the deck is further stacked against them.

The rise in high-poverty neighborhoods has been greatest in smaller metro areas. This goes hand in hand with the recent rise of suburban poverty. As inner cities become gentrified and rents rise, the poor gravitate to cheaper quarters in the suburbs. The white middle class move to suburbs farther out—or back to the cities themselves, replacing the displaced poor.

The suburbs have few educational, employment, or health programs for low-income families. Jobs are scattered and public transportation is poor. This is a whole new set of problems, as the incidence of suburban poverty outpaces growth of poverty in the urban centers.

Far too many children in America live lives of hunger, stress, exclusion from play and the normal activities of childhood, physical and psychological damage, and inescapable pessimism. Their future opportunities are severely reduced, as we shall further document.

CHAPTER 3

AMERICAN ATTITUDES TOWARD POVERTY

Despite the intensity of child suffering and disadvantage in America, the nation seems unwilling and unable to do what's necessary to minimize it. The reasons have a long history.

WARRING CAMPS

Two warring ideological camps in America have battled over the causes of poverty since the early 1800s. They are at either end of a spectrum. The *individualist* camp argues that people bring poverty on themselves. Society or the economy is only minimally to blame; human behavior is the main culprit. The *economic and institutional* camp, often called *structuralist*, argues that the main causes of poverty are lack of jobs, lack of political power, and racial prejudice. I'd argue, in between, is a third camp, composed of those who believe in a "culture of poverty," which can in turn be caused by both behavior and institutional structures.

For the most part, the individualist camp has dominated the discourse and held political influence in America. In this view, the "deserving" poor are the sick, the elderly, and children. The "undeserving" poor are the able-bodied, which is why society owes them little or no aid. America was the land of opportunity, and the poor didn't work hard enough to take advantage of it. For a time, particularly for white farmers and homeowners, the land's generosity seemed to make the dream real, especially in contrast to life in the Old World. Until the rise of wealthy European social democracies, American wages were virtually always higher than in the Old World, though they were far from generous.

Despite this long-prevailing American view, the structuralist camp has occasionally gained power over the course of history. Constructive compromises on aid to the poor were sometimes reached. Strong intellectual counterarguments to the individualist argument came from the left, particularly after the Industrial Revolution, the depression of the 1890s and the rise of the Robber Barons, the Great Depression of the 1930s, and during the Great Society and War on Poverty of the 1960s. Regulations on abusive labor practices were adopted and government supports of income were created, such as pensions for mothers in the early 1900s. Later, cash welfare was established under FDR and expanded under Lyndon Johnson.

But for the most part, individualist arguments ruled, which fit neatly with classist, racist, elitist, and some religious attitidues. It also fit neatly with businesses' arguments about damaging government interference and obstacles to efficiency and growth.

The turn to the individualist attitude to the poor came as early as the 1800s. In England, the Elizabethan Poor Law of 1601 had endorsed the disbursement of state relief under certain circumstances. "But by the early nineteenth century," writes the historian Walter Trattner, "industrial capitalism, urbanization, greater poverty, higher taxes, and the laissez-faire philosophy had made the pursuit and accumulation of wealth a moral virtue and dependency a vice." Benjamin Disraeli, the British prime minister, maintained it was a crime to be poor. "Poor relief was redesigned to increase fear of insecurity, rather than to check its causes or even to alleviate its problems," Trattner argues.

America followed suit, trumpeting its individualism and faith in self-reliance. Ralph Waldo Emerson, who wrote his famous essay "Self-Reliance" in 1841, was its eloquent ambassador. Biblical injunctions were now reinterpreted as the Second Great Awakening glorified the personal value of diligence.

The first major modern economic recession struck America in 1819. By 1821, despite bad times for so many, the New York Society for the Prevention of Pauperism wrote, "No man who is temperate, frugal, and willing to work need suffer or become a pauper for want of employment." One so-called reformer said that the "sober and able-bodied, if industriously disposed, cannot long want employment. They cannot, but in their own folly and vices, long remain indigent."

Poorhouses and workhouses were started across the country, which were more demanding than solicitous. The able-bodied were generally put to demanding work.

One objective was to make the workhouse so harsh and demeaning that it kept individuals in the labor market.

Dependency became a serious concern of some poverty skeptics—as it did so vividly in the 1990s in the United States during arguments about welfare reform.

PROGRESSIVISM

As prosperity increased in the later 1800s, a progressive wave of private social reformers arose to replace ineffective government programs. Partly this was spurred by well-educated women who had discovered this role while tending to the casualties of the Civil War. Poor children's welfare became a particular focus partly because there were so many children in poverty in this period, many more than in other age groups.

A pioneering psychologist, G. Stanley Hall, studied the development of the child closely in *Adolescence*, a book published in 1904 and a worthy predecessor to the voluminous work done in our era. The attention led to a variety of solutions to aid poor children. Children were put in separate almshouses from their parents; new institutions were created for them, including eventually juvenile centers; and a court system for young "delinquents" was created. On balance, these early attempts to protect and nourish children were efforts mostly gone wrong.

Late in the nineteenth century, as the economy prospered, new efforts to relieve poverty began. In particular, settlement houses were established across the country. Among the leaders of the movement was Jane Addams, the founder of Chicago's Hull House. A wave of college-educated women and men became social reformers in these years, a kind of Peace Corps of the times. Social workers, nurses, doctors, college students, and teachers fed and educated the immigrant and urban poor in these settlement houses. These reformers were less interested in pure charity than their earlier colleagues and more in development and improvement of the poor.

In the 1890s, the nation suffered its most severe recession of the century. Destitution could not easily be ignored. Fear of a socialist political wave was now a driving force. Muckraking journalists and authors were writing about business abuse, government corruption, and the squalor of life in New York City's Lower East Side and other quarters of the city. Protests and violence marked these decades, in particular with the growth of the unions. A wave of immigrants congregated in the cities, some 14 million between 1860 and 1900 and another 9 million from 1900 to 1910.

Out of these conditions grew one of those moments in American history when the tide turned markedly in favor of the poor—up to a point. The low level of wages was more openly recognized, and unions were gaining supporters. Robert Hunter wrote in his influential 1904 book *Poverty*, "Many, many thousand families receive wages so inadequate that no care in spending . . . will make them suffice for the family needs." He claimed there were 10 million poor in America, 12 percent of the population.

In 1912, a group of settlement house workers compiled a list of requirements for a decent society, which, as the historian Mike Wallace recounts, included "an eight-hour day, a six-day week, abolition of tenement manufacture, establishment of occupational health and safety standards, prohibition of child labor, regulation of women's employment, and provision of federal insurance against accidents, illness, unemployment, and old age." These policies were adopted into Theodore Roosevelt's Progressive Party presidential platform in that same year, an unprecedented welfare platform for a major political party. On the convention floor, Jane Addams seconded Teddy's nomination, saying that "the new party has become the American exponent of a world-wide movement toward juster social conditions, a movement which the United States, lagging behind other great nations, has been unaccountably slow to embody in political action."

But American poverty skepticism retained influence. Regulations were adopted to establish standards for wages and hours for some workers, and to minimize child labor. Public health programs were created and free public education was expanded. A federal Children's Bureau was proposed by TR in 1909 and established in 1912. But social security, health insurance, and unemployment insurance were not passed, though some European nations had adopted some of these programs in the late 1800s, led by the Kaiser in Prussia, who himself was warding off socialist pressure.

Some of the new progressive programs were reversed or stymied in the conservative 1920s, but the

Depression that gripped the nation led to sweeping regulatory, social insurance, and jobs programs in the 1930s.

THE NEW DEAL

Franklin Roosevelt was a small-government advocate as governor of New York State, but as unemployment soared, his rapid shift to bold experimental reforms was stunning. Over several years, the New Deal included Wall Street regulation, Social Security, bank deposit insurance, unemployment insurance, welfare programs for the poor, direct public-sector job creation, labor organizing laws, and more, in a wide and deep transformation of American society. Sometimes forgotten, though, is that the New Deal was also restrained in scope by deep-seated, long-standing American attitudes about limits on government and the fear of fostering dependency among the poor and workers.

In particular, the New Deal did not include universal health insurance, an integral part of the new social safety net of European nations, which would have been beneficial not only to the poor but all Americans. Also, Social Security benefits were meager by later standards, not a true retirement income, and they did not cover workers in agriculture and housework, many of whom were black. In fact, there were restrictions on the number of blacks allowed to participate in the Civilian Conservation Corps (CCC), a jobs program for men. In 1933, only 5 percent of CCC workers were black, and only 6 percent the next year. Robert Fechner, the head of the CCC, "let it be known that black enrollment would compose no more than 10 percent." The CCC was also almost completely segregated into white and black units; indeed, segregation was the norm in most federally funded programs through the Second World War and into the era of the GI Bill. Mortgages to blacks subsidized under the Home Ownership Loan Corporation were also limited. And children always bore the injustices done to their parents.

Harry Truman also failed to get a national health insurance program passed. Strong lobbying pressure, particularly from the American Medical Association, was aligned against it. In the following eight years under Republican Dwight Eisenhower, social programs were expanded modestly, including Social Security and unemployment insurance, but Ike, who feared inflation and leaned toward small government, was determined not to be a big spender or to expand the New Deal significantly. His national highway system was a major infrastructure program that provided many jobs, but it was sold to the public as a national security program in the early years of the Cold War.

THE WAR ON POVERTY

The War on Poverty of the 1960s did not find its impetus during the economic straits of deep depression, unlike the previous major waves of progressive inroads against inadequate poverty policy. In fact, the national economy was prospering. Civil rights demonstrations and free speech protests began to rock American society during the 1950s and early 1960s and grew rapidly in the latter half of the 1960s. Urban riots erupted in the mid-1960s in Watts, Los Angeles, and in Detroit. But the national economy was prospering.

There had been ongoing concerns with what many considered inadequate social policies throughout the 1950s. Ike, who vetoed several major programs, was criticized by the left. But public consciousness about poverty did not seem fully provoked until the publication of Michael Harrington's book *The Other America: Poverty in the United States*. Harrington asserted that 25 percent of all Americans, as noted, were poor at a time when the nation thought it had solved its deepest economic problems, roughly 50 million Americans. The book shocked America and became an overnight bestseller. Until Harrington, wrote the social critic Dwight McDonald in an early 1963 *New Yorker* article, "almost everybody has assumed that because of the New Deal's social legislation and—more important—the prosperity we have enjoyed since 1940, mass poverty no longer exists in this country."

The Other America arrived just as the civil rights movement had forced the questions of equality and inclusion in the postwar boom front and center in the American mind. Americans seemed prepared to fight social problems again after the Eisenhower hiatus. Harrington had helped to publicize and recast the debate, just as the outspoken investigative journalists—the "muckrakers" of the late 1800s and early 1900s—helped shape public opinion, and as analytical studies seemed to influence policymakers in the Great Depression.

Left-wing literature in the 1950s and 1960s molded a changing political era and had a lasting impact. Among the most influential books were *Silent Spring* by Rachel Carson, *The Feminine Mystique* by Betty Friedan, *I Know Why the Caged Bird Sings* by Maya Angelou, *Giovanni's Room* by James Baldwin, *Unsafe At Any Speed* by Ralph Nader, and, earlier, *Invisible Man* by Ralph Ellison. These brought literary persuasion to bear on key issues of a newly liberal nation: anti-racism, environmentalism, feminism, and corporate responsibility.

Harrington's book was among the biggest sellers and most influential works of the time. In the 1950s and early 1960s, America had been more concerned with problems of an affluent and technologically advancing society: the ennui and conformity in the prosperous suburbs; overt and ostentatious materialism; the immorality of advertising; changing sexual mores; and the threat of nuclear war.

The notion that one-third of Americans were undernourished and without decent housing in 1937, as Roosevelt had reported, was one thing. It was, after all, the Great Depression (the actual poverty rate was closer to two-thirds then). By the 1950s, most Americans, however, had risen out of poverty, and many of those who did so seemed to assume that anyone able and willing could do so as well. America was now economically overconfident, and on balance accepted the claim that the New Deal had mitigated the effects of the cruel side of capitalism.

While there was a rising demand to expand civil rights, John F. Kennedy's chief economist, Walter Heller, was concerned that poverty had not fallen more rapidly as the nation's economy had grown in the post–World War II era. And it was worst for minorities. Heller gave Harrington's book to Kennedy, among other reports on poverty, inspiring the president, and perhaps even more his brother, Robert, the attorney general. Reducing high incidence of poverty became a national priority.

Soon after Lyndon Johnson became president, the White House called Harrington to Washington to help advise on the War on Poverty. Harrington worked with Kennedy in-law Sargent Shriver, among others, at the new Office of Economic Opportunity.

The Harvard economist John Kenneth Galbraith, who had worked for Roosevelt during the New Deal, had published a best-selling book, *The Affluent Society*, in 1958. Its title was widely misunderstood. Galbraith's book was about the failures of prosperity rather than its successes, and it, too, had helped spur the renewed progressivism of the sixties. Among other matters of public neglect, Galbraith discussed poverty in a fresh way, emphasizing that with economic recovery and a rising middle class, poverty nevertheless persisted. He no doubt also influenced Walter Heller and his personal friend President Kennedy.

Galbraith, however, had seriously underestimated the number of poor, falling victim to the consistent underestimation of poverty by researchers and policy-makers. Four years later, the more realistic if still not fully accurate number publicized by Harrington alarmed the nation partly because the notable progressive Galbraith had accepted earlier government estimates, despite his novel and important work on social issues. (A number of scholars estimated poverty at rates far higher than Galbraith did in the later 1950s.)

Harrington had settled on a consensus value of $3,000 as an annual poverty line, though some reputable analysts were proposing it should be $3,500 a year or higher. Harrington's poverty line resulted in the poverty rate of 25 percent, compared to Galbraith's "one family in thirteen," under 8 percent, based on a $1,000 poverty line.

Harrington, the frumpy, earnestly committed social worker, while partially correcting the urbane Ivy Leaguer Galbraith, also praised him. He wrote in *The Other America*, "Even given these disagreements with Galbraith, his achievement is considerable. He was one of the first to understand that there are enough poor people in the United States to constitute a sub-culture of misery, but not enough of them to challenge the conscience and the imagination of the nation." In the Depression, by contrast, there had been more than enough.

They both agreed a political movement was needed to assure social justice because, as Galbraith argued, economic growth by itself would not eradicate poverty. "I would agree with Galbraith," Harrington went on, "that poverty in the sixties has qualities that give it a hardiness in the face of affluence heretofore unknown. As documented and described in his book, there were many special factors keeping the unskilled workers, the minorities, the agricultural poor, and the aged in a culture of poverty. If there is to be a way out, it will come from human action, from political change, not from automatic processes."

Harrington's book helped provoke the first major federal response to poverty since the Great Depression. Lyndon Johnson's War on Poverty, which he declared in his 1964 State of the Union address, began that year with the Economic Opportunity Act—a name that promised something different from direct poverty reduction. Johnson, mindful of conservative views, insisted he wasn't offering an "opiate" but "opportunity." The War on Poverty included Head Start, the Job Corps, federal funds for schools in poor neighborhoods, and an idealistic community action proposal to enable communities to establish their own poverty policies. Johnson also made food stamps permanent by law in a decade in which widespread starvation, particularly in the South, came to national notice partly through the efforts of Bobby Kennedy.

Johnson's Great Society programs cannot be separated from the War on Poverty. In them, he expanded Social Security benefits and started Medicare for senior citizens and Medicaid for the poor. There had been efforts in various states to develop retirement programs for seniors; now there was an umbrella federal plan. These were bold forays. His extraordinary civil rights efforts—the Civil Rights Act and the Voting Rights Act—to outlaw racist discrimination, among other aspects of Jim Crow, were effectively an antipoverty program as well.

The renewed progressive attitude on poverty under LBJ extended in some ways directly from FDR's New Deal. Aid to Families with Dependent Children (AFDC), the cash welfare program for the poor that was started under FDR in 1935, was sharply expanded in the 1960s to include black mothers, who had been largely restricted from aid originally. The changes made to AFDC were the consequences of organized activists as well as poliycmakers.

Optimism momentarily abounded, and Johnson's adviser Sargent Shriver argued that the country should set a goal of eradicating poverty by 1976.

THE HISTORY OF THE ABSOLUTE AMERICAN POVERTY LINE

America chose to adopt an absolute poverty line as its official measure of poverty in 1969 based on the work of a dedicated analyst in the Social Security Administration, Mollie Orshansky. She did not believe the new measure, a line beneath which a family could not subsist, was an adequate measure of the poor in America, but its simplicity appealed to lawmakers—and because it was low, it held down federal costs.

Thus, the decision to adopt an absolute poverty line that would never change was made out of expediency. It was only adjusted upward to account for inflation, not rising average or median incomes. The poverty historian Alice O'Connor notes that an absolute line would also make it possible to give the appearance of reducing poverty quickly. A relative line, measured as a proportion of median incomes, would always show that some poverty existed.

The well-meaning Orshansky decided to compute her poverty line based on estimates of a minimal food budget. Nutritional analyses were often the basis of poverty estimates. She focused on the surveys by the Department of Agriculture completed in the mid-1950s of money spent on food. With estimates of two food budgets, one very low and another somewhat higher, she then decided to multiply them by three to arrive at a poverty line.

Multiplying by three would supposedly compensate for other needs, including housing, electricity, transportation, and clothing. The multiple of three was based on a nineteenth-century analysis by a German social reformer, Ernest Engels (no relation to Friedrich Engels, Karl Marx's co-author), who found that the poorer a family was, the higher the proportion of income it spent on food. A low-income family, calculated Engels, usually spent about one-third of its income on food.

By the 1960s and 1970s, poor families spent a lesser proportion on food—but needed four or five times their food budget for other needs, according to contemporary studies. This fact the Johnson administration ignored.

Orshansky's poverty line was proposed in a report in 1963 and again in 1965, when it came to $3,128 a year. This was roughly the same as the poverty line used by the Kennedy Council of Economic Advisers led by Walter Heller, partly based on the work done by CEA economist Robert Lampman. The $3,000 figure, the historian Gordon Fisher concluded, was a consensus at the time. It was also roughly the level of income of a full-time worker earning the minimum wage, and about the highest welfare payment made by a state. As Fisher notes, it was also the level at which a family of four would start paying income taxes. Several different analyses yielded a poverty threshold of about the same amount.

This is, of course, no way to establish a poverty line. The miscalculation is especially upsetting because it came at a time when concern for the poor had become politically intense and action was being taken. Orshansky, meaning well, at least made adjustments for the size of the family. She had been concerned that a one-size-fits-all computation would result in undercounting poor children.

Few believed that a poverty line could be stagnant and still keep pace with growing prosperity and economic changes. The economist Oscar Ornati, after examining poverty lines drawn by reformers, unionists, and economists since 1905, noted that levels were increased substantially every decade or two. He concluded that analysts realized that poor people needed their real incomes to increase over time just to live at subsistence or near-subsistence levels. Adjustments for inflation weren't nearly enough. The fact that today's Official Poverty Measure has not been adjusted in a serious way for fifty years is a scandal.

Even the conservative economist Rose Friedman, the wife of Milton Friedman, favored raising the line periodically. Orshansky was concerned, writing as early as 1963, "As the general level of living moves upward and expands beyond [current] necessities[,] the standards of what constitutes an irreducible minimum change." A few years later she wrote, "The difficulties in setting the poverty line are increased when the definition is to be used to measure progress over a span of time. Statistical nicety will be better served if the criterion selected remains invariant. The realities of everyday living suggest it cannot be—at least not for very long. Though the change in consumption patterns from any one year to the next might be minuscule, over the long run[,] the upgrading that goes with the developing United States economy will be too great to be ignored."

Robert Ball, long the respected commissioner of Social Security, joined the debate, writing in 1965, "Measures of income adequacy (or of poverty) change over time with the rise in general levels of living." Ball argued that "one of the most difficult methodological questions we will have to face in the next few years is when and how to adjust the definition of poverty."

This opinion was widespread. A colleague of Ball's wrote in 1967, "It is easy to observe that poverty in the U.S. today cannot meaningfully be defined in the same way as in the U.S. of 1900.... It is more difficult to project forward when and by what amounts the measure of poverty will need to be changed in the future. Yet obviously today's measure, even if corrected year by year for changes in the price level—the purchasing power of money—should not be acceptable twenty, ten or perhaps even five years hence."

Despite this consensus on what became known as "the elasticity of poverty," the Johnson administration chose not to adopt a measure that would be adjusted periodically.

There were other examples of Johnson administration stinginess when it came to the poor. Orshansky and others urged the administration to adopt the higher food budget estimates made by the Agriculture Department in 1965, replacing those of 1955. Such a change would have raised the poverty line by 8 percent, adding more than one million people to the numbers of the officially poor. The Office of Economic Opportunity had just started using the original OPM as a basis for determining benefits in 1965, and fine-tuning might easily have been accomplished. But the Johnson administration was averse to raising the cost of these social programs, not wanting to incur further ire from conservatives.

In the same years that the inadequate Official Poverty Measure (OPM) was developed and implemented, the federal government spent $168 billion (more than $950 billion in today's terms) to send young and poor Americans to fight in the Vietnam War. When Johnson and the Democratic Congress made war spending a cornerstone of the budget, they also refused to raise benefits to cover all the poor.

Little analysis was done in the 1960s and early 1970s to understand how the OPM would affect children. The Johnson administration refused to adopt adjustments to the OPM based on the size of families, considering it too cumbersome.

THE SPM: WELL-MEANING BUT INADEQUATE REFORM

The failure to account for the elasticity of poverty had serious consequences for the poor. When adopted, the OPM was about 50 percent of typical family incomes (the median). The OPM, raised only with inflation and pegged to the Consumer Price Index, thus kept falling as a percentage of growing American incomes. By 1990, the OPM was only 40 percent of median family incomes, and today it stands at only 30 percent. The nation and its media rarely acknowledge this decline. To announce that 17.5 percent of children are poor based on such a low poverty line is meaningless.

In the 1990s, a group of experts from various fields was organized by Congress under the auspices of the National Academy of Sciences to propose serious reforms to the OPM.

A major new computational issue had arisen as the social programs adopted and expanded since the 1990s were dominated by tax credits. These included the Earned Income Tax Credit (EITC) and the Child Tax Credit (CTC). Taxes owed are reduced according to one's income on a falling scale. Because tax credits are not cash, they were not added to the income of the poor when calculating the official poverty line. The increasingly important food stamp program had similarly been uncounted because it was not cash, as was the case with the special nutritional assistance program for Women, Infants, and Children (WIC) and a number of other programs. Conservatives and others therefore claimed that poverty rates were in reality much lower than claimed by the Census Bureau, and that millions of children were incorrectly counted as poor.

The Supplemental Poverty Measure (SPM) was partly created to take account of the tax credits. The SPM counts income after taxes and therefore includes the benefits of the EITC and other tax credits in measuring income for the poor. It also includes SNAP. But unlike the OPM, which counts pre-tax income, the SPM subtracts income taxes and payroll taxes from income.

In formulating the SPM, the experts finally agreed that an absolute poverty line was misleading. They based the Supplemental Poverty Measure not only on food but on a package of needs including housing, clothing, and electricity, calculated by taking the average amount of money families spent over the most recent five-year period. The average would change each year: the latest year's spending would be incorporated, the furthest back discarded. Thus, it was a quasi-relative poverty line—unlike the absolute official poverty line.

The creators of the SPM also believed certain out-of-pocket purchases made by the poor should be included as deductions from income. These were cash medical care outlays, especially large for the elderly, as well as costs associated with work, such as childcare and transportation expenses.

While on the face of it, this seems a more generous

recognition of the needs of the poor, it, too, is biased. It deducts only the cash the poor can afford to pay. Young low-income adults cannot pay very much for childcare, for example, especially compared to the middle class, so their incomes are not reduced very much when calculating poverty. Child poverty, as the scholar Shawn Fremstad argues, is seriously understated by the supplemental measure for this reason, even as overall poverty rose. Meanwhile, elderly poverty shoots up under the SPM because their cash medical outlays are so high.

The SPM also adjusts for the cost of housing geographically, which has the odd result of reducing poverty in high-poverty rural areas because prices are low. Few believe these are accurate assessments of poverty by region.

Defying the expectations of conservatives and others, when the supplemental measure was officially published by the Census Bureau for the first time in 2011, the poverty rate under the SPM did not fall but *rose* above the official measure, though only a percentage point or two. The national supplemental poverty income threshold for a non-homeowning family of four was $27,005 in 2017 versus $24,858 under the OPM. There were nearly 1.3 million more poor Americans under the SPM measure.

A more sensible way of measuring poverty might have been a direct relative measure—as a percentage of typical incomes, as is done in Europe. Then we would have a higher poverty line that would, at the same time, measure the proportion of all income the poor earn— a social reform with a built-in mechanism for gauging how economically equal our society is at any given time.

It is no surprise, then, that the official poverty line at the beginning of the Great Society was roughly half of typical incomes, but it fell in value to 30 percent over time because of the way it was constructed. The Johnson administration feared adopting too high a line because it would raise the cost of expanding social programs, riling political opponents and upsetting hierarchies of class, race, and gender in the United States. The Great Society's poverty rate—the OPM—was made official in 1969 under President Richard Nixon, a man who worried little that the poverty line was too low.

CHAPTER 4

THE ANTI-WELFARE
POLICY CONSENSUS

A new dominating point of view—a revival of traditional American poverty attitudes—emerged in the mid-1970s to replace the Rooseveltian social philosophy. Concerned that these poverty and income support programs made recipients of benefits dependent on government, many Americans eventually decided that such programs must include work requirements. Outright cash grants became a diminished part of the American response to poverty, a radical shift reflecting the rise again of the individualistic philosophy with its victim-blaming poverty theories.

American poverty policy thus shifted away from the Johnson-era War on Poverty. The crowning achievement for the individualists was the reform of the welfare program, culminating in 1996 with the adoption of Temporary Assistance for Needy Families, or TANF. The law itself was cannily called the Personal Responsibility and Work Opportunity Reconciliation Act (PRWORA).

The new program, replacing Johnson's welfare policies and Franklin Roosevelt's program for poor families, established work requirements for all who received benefits. The original welfare policy had distributed cash to the needy with children without such conditions. TANF eventually covered only one-third as many families as did Aid for Families with Dependent Children. As the centerpiece of change in social philosophy, the welfare battle will be reviewed in more detail in the next chapter.

In the meantime, other major social welfare policies involving children were adopted, reshaping the American safety net.

TAX CREDITS AND TRANSFERS

The Earned Income Tax Credit, originally a Republican program started in 1975 under President Gerald Ford, has been made more generous over the years and is now one of the nation's major social programs. It provides a credit against income taxes based on a family's earnings; the percentage of income taxed falls as the family income rises, up to a maxium. Benefits were increased in the 1980s, most significantly in 1993, and increased again in 2009 during the Great Recession. The benefits are available to all working families with children, and more recently, a small benefit was made available to individuals.

The EITC is a particular favorite of liberals seeking to expand the safety net. Congressman Ro Khanna, for example, has proposed doubling benefits for families and raising them for working individuals. This tax expenditure (i.e., the amount of tax revenue forgone due to the tax credit) now provides more than $60 billion in benefits to families with children. Across the political spectrum, its great value is seen as encouraging lower-income Americans to work, a view supported by considerable evidence. Another singular political advantage: the benefits don't show up in the federal budget as a direct expenditure. The original welfare program in America, Aid to Families with Dependent Children, reduced payments substantially as people worked more. The AFDC welfare program, for all the anger it aroused, was relatively small and declined in cost from a high of $26 billion in 1976 to $20.4 billion in 1996.

Meanwhile, the Earned Income Tax Credit program grew, and so did the number of families receiving it. In 2017, about 44 percent of families with children received benefits from the EITC. The maximum was $3,400 for a family with one child and $5,616 for a family with two children. The average benefit across America was more than $3,000. The benefits diminish gradually at higher incomes, falling to no benefits for families with one child at an income of $40,320, and $49,194 for families with three or more children.

A similar tax credit for families with children was adopted in 1996, the Child Tax Credit (CTC). Together these programs have raised 8.9 million people above the supplemental poverty line, including 4.8 million children.

The Child Tax Credit works similarly to the EITC. It is a $2,000 tax credit per child to all working families with children; it phases out at higher income levels, beginning at $200,000 for an individual or $400,000 for married couples filing jointly. President Trump's tax bill dramatically expanded access to the CTC for wealthy families; previously, the tax credit had started to phase out at $75,000 for single filers or $110,000 for married couples filing jointly. In 2017, the program cost the federal government about $50 billion in forgone tax revenues; in 2018, it cost $104 billion (after the Trump boost for higher-income families).

These two programs combined are the largest anti-poverty programs for children, aside from Medicaid, under the current policy regime. Research shows most of the benefits go to Americans whose wages are high enough to qualify for the full tax credits. A single parent with two children with an annual income of $10,000 received a $4,010 earned income credit in 2019—but the same parent with twice the income would have received $5,616. This disparity is also built in to the Child Tax Credit. Poor families with no tax liability received only a $1,400 credit per child—in order to qualify for the full $2,000 credit, families had to earn at least $12,000 a year. For those whose tax liability is less than their credit, part of the credit is refunded in cash. The same is true of the EITC. This refundability feature is critical to providing some aid to very low-income families. Nevertheless, "welfare reform and the decline in unconditional cash assistance is fully felt by those with the lowest incomes," write scholars Hilary Hoynes and Diane Schanzenbach. "More than half of the increased spending for the EITC and more than three-quarters of the increased spending for the CTC goes to those with income between 100-200% of [the] poverty [line]." There is a congressional movement to make more of the benefit refundable to those with very low incomes.

There are other important programs that aid children, including food stamps, Medicaid, housing subsidies, and TANF. In total, federal spending on children (including the EITC and the CTC) comes to roughly $481 billion today, down from $516 billion in 2010. In 1990, all programs for children came to roughly $110 billion in today's dollars. It's clear that what America has done for poor children is not meager. But many millions of American children continue to live in poverty. There is much further to go.

The poverty rate for children as measured by the SPM is down from 28.4 percent in 1967 to 15.6 percent in 2017 by one measure favored by many progressives. This comes to about 45 percent, according to a methodology adopted by a Columbia University group of scholars as requested by the Obama CEA. Other progressives believe the methodology overstates the decline. It assumes, for example, that the group of products that defines poverty is the same in 1993 or 1998 as in 2010. The Columbia group used a more conventional methodology in an earlier report that some economists and sociologists, also progressive in intellectual bent, think is more accurate. It yields a decline of far less, some 20 to 25 percent. This reduction is welcome, of course, but not nearly as dramatic as when using the more dubious methodology. Either way, the poverty rate for children is still very high by international standards.

WHY A HIGH CHILD POVERTY RATE

A 15 to 17.5 percent child poverty rate, depending on the measures used, leaves the United States well above the levels for peer nations. For decades—from 1960 through 2017—all federal spending on children (including all tax credits, and even the exemption for dependents) rose but has remained no higher than about 2 to 3 percent of GDP. By contrast, federal spending on the elderly grew to 7.1 percent of GDP in 2013 and is more than 9.3 percent of GDP today—much of it Social Security and Medicare. When adjusted for inflation, one recent study notes, "federal spending on the elderly between 1960 and 2017 increased . . . from about $4,000 to about $29,000" per elderly person. Over this same period, federal spending on children rose from about $300 to only $4,800 per child, up by 16 times. (Keep in mind that GDP was roughly $500 billion in 1960 compared to $20 trillion today, up by forty times.)

Some note that the elderly poverty rate under the newer supplemental measure has risen substantially, but this is misleading, due in large part to the relatively large medical cash payments of the elderly, which are now deducted from their income to compute poverty rates.

We have been discussing only Washington's role in antipoverty programs for children and the elderly. State and local spending is much higher for children, due to public education funding, than it is for the elderly. But even so, overall spending on the elderly per person in America, federal and state, is still about two and a half times that for children. This does not mean elderly social spending should be cut. Rather, child welfare should be raised.

It can be done. For a sense of scale and priorities, consider the tax credits and exemptions America now favors as the social policy of choice. Some $1.7 trillion in tax revenues is forgone annually by the federal government's benefits for middle- and upper-class Americans: tax breaks such as the mortgage interest rate deduction and the deduction to corporations for providing health insurance to their employees. This is to say, current tax expenditures for children come to *less than a tenth* of what the federal government spends on middle-class and wealthy Americans every year.

WHO IS GETTING THE MONEY?

America spends hundreds of billions of dollars on poor children, but is the aid getting to those who need it most? A valuable study by Hilary Hoynes and Diane Schanzenbach, based on what people spend, underscores such concerns. The key finding of Hoynes and Schanzenbach's carefully adjusted data is that social spending to officially poor families with children fell from 87 percent of social spending in 1990 to 56 percent in 2015. The programs they included in their calculation are Medicaid, the EITC, the CTC, SNAP, housing assistance, and the original cash welfare program, Aid to Families with Dependent Children, along with its "workfare" successor, TANF (Temporary Assistance to Needy Families).

They write, "In 1992, welfare reform has not yet occurred, the EITC is quite small, there is no CTC, and the benefits are targeted at the bottom of the earnings distribution. In 2015, in contrast, TANF is no longer an entitlement (so excluded here), the EITC has expanded, the CTC has been introduced, and SNAP remained much the same. On net, resources have shifted away from the lowest earnings levels and moved up the income distribution."

Reform policies in the 1990s thus marked a major turning point in social welfare policy in America. The victims are the poorest and children. Hoynes and Schanzenbach corroborate this in convincing detail—and with hard data. They write, "within the funds that are allocated to children, there have been substantial shifts over the past 20 years," namely, that "an increasing share is going to children near and above the poverty threshold, while a decreasing share is directed to the poorest children living below the poverty threshold despite a relatively stable share of children living in poverty."

Because a larger proportion of African American families live below the poverty line, these policies have in particular damaged them. Hoynes and Schanzenbach also argue strongly that these work-dependent policies make the poor, and their children, particularly vulnerable during recessions when unemployment rises. Only if the federal government responds by raising SNAP distribution levels and unemployment insurance coverage, as did President Obama in the recent Great Recession, is hardship mitigated.

It is time we look back to the War on Poverty's direct cash transfer models as an alternative.

HOW DID THE WAR ON POVERTY FARE?

Given America's cynical attitudes about helping the poor, it's not surprising that policymakers and others appear to leap at any opportunity to claim that Johnson's antipoverty programs failed, and even made poverty worse. But Ronald Reagan's 1983 comment that there'd been a War on Poverty "which poverty won" was nonsense. The official poverty rate—the proportion of all people who fell below the newly established poverty line—was 22.4 percent in 1959, some 40 million people. It fell to 11.1 percent in 1973, declining to 25 million people. Rapid economic growth at first and then the Johnson policies were the sources of the quick success. Elderly poverty fell most rapidly as a result of increased Social Security payments, but child poverty fell almost as sharply, along with family poverty.

During the War on Poverty and in its immediate wake, many believed that the nation was making adequate progress in dealing with the age-old scourge. But progress slowed. During the next forty-five years, the number of people living below the OPM never dropped below 11 percent, and rose as high as 15 percent. The number of officially poor increased to nearly 40 million under Reagan and George H. W. Bush—a period of high unemployment and stagnating wage growth. Reagan was determined to turn back Great Society programs, and he partly succeeded, for instance, cutting back on food stamp benefits. Child poverty rates under the non-official SPM by one computation rose as high as 30 percent under Reagan—and 20 percent of children were officially poor in 1989.

The official rate fell again during the economic boom under Bill Clinton, but the number of all poor rose sharply to 45 million with the Great Recession of 2008. It is currently around 43 million, with a 12.3 percent official poverty rate—never returning to 11 percent. As a reminder, 17.5 percent of children are officially poor in America today.

The most heartening result of the War on Poverty was its success in dealing with extreme poverty and starvation. The Field Foundation, an arm of the Chicago retailing family, had sent medical observers to the Deep South to investigate reports of starvation in May 1967. They found rare disease like marasmus and kwashiorkor as well as rickets and other indicators of severe malnutrition. Peter Edelman and Robert Kennedy had gone down earlier together and witnessed the severe starvation. In 1968, a CBS television documentary showed a newborn die of malnutrition on camera.

In 1977, ten years later, a Field Foundation team returned and found a huge improvement. One physician, a member of the team, reported, "It is not possible any more to find very easily the bloated bellies, the shriveled infants, the gross evidence of vitamin and protein deficiencies in children that we identified in the late 1960s." It was clear evidence that social programs mattered.

A SECOND ROUND OF ANTIPOVERTY EFFORTS

The poverty skeptics never disappeared. Government spending on the Vietnam War and a growing federal budget deficit slowed aid. Those new antipoverty measures that were implemented increasingly hewed to the emerging policy consensus, premised on the individualist school of thought, on minimizing welfare spending and the social rights of the poor. Nixon proposed a guaranteed income for families with children, though he wanted to reduce conventional cash welfare. President Carter proposed a guaranteed income several years later. Both proposals were defeated by Congress, reflecting skepticism of poverty policies, especially if they involved cash welfare.

Other programs did pass, however. One was the Supplemental Security Income Program, which provided cash benefits for very low-income individuals over sixty-five and for blind and disabled adults. Another new cash program targeted women, infants, and children at risk of nutritional deprivation (WIC). Food stamps were made available to those who made under 130 percent of the poverty line, and food stamp benefits were made more generous. Originally, participants had to buy food stamps, but in 1977 a law was passed to do away with that requirement, enabling them to spread to the poorest regions, where they had not been widely distributed. Reagan reduced taxes for low-income workers and expanded Medicaid, but, as a reminder, he cut spending on food stamps and other programs.

Never to be suppressed for long, the individualist school of thought regained the political and theoretical upper hand in the 1990s in the battle to reform welfare. It was to be the new age of tax-oriented social policies and work requirements—buttressed by questionable behaviorist models for understanding the origins of poverty, and a "culture of poverty" argument that became widely shared across the mainstream political spectrum, the punditry, and the academy by the 1980s.

CHAPTER 5

THE "CULTURE OF POVERTY"

The "culture of poverty" as an explanatory mechanism for the persistence of poverty first gained currency when the sociologist Oscar Lewis, writing about Mexico, Puerto Rico, and Spanish-speaking New York City in the 1960s, proposed that a culture of bad habits existed in these countries. The poor develop norms of behavior that keep them poor, he argued, including easily tapped frustration and an inability to delay gratification, and Lewis believed these habits are passed on to the following generations, hardening a wall around the poor.

The lure of this kind of thinking is clear. Kaaryn Gustafson, a professor of law at the University of California, Irvine, put it well in 2014: "The appeal of the 'culture of poverty' is that it offers a clear explanation for poverty, an explanation that removes both individual agency and collective responsibility from the equation. This simplistic account of poverty—one that suggests that certain populations have developed settled social and economic sub-cultures outside the mainstream—blinds us from the historical contingencies and the political decisions that have led to a high rate of poverty relative to most wealthy nations."

The culture of poverty as an idea equates with the notion of otherness that the historian Alice O'Connor alludes to when she observes, "The myth of otherness associated with being poor in America persists and cuts across ideological lines." It fits especially well with the American attitude of blaming the poor for their condition.

Blacks in particular, it was widely argued, had a "subculture" apart from the mainstream of America. They belonged to an "underclass." Poverty could be remedied if black men found the will to be responsible and work hard and break out of the cultural trap. It could be reduced if black women did not marry so early or have out-of-wedlock children. Unfortunately, liberals partook of this view—indeed, among them the most talented of writers on the left—by joining the right in demands for work requirements and the virtual end of unrestricted cash welfare.

Ken Auletta wrote a book called *The Underclass* in 1982, in which he asserted that ghetto life is "utterly different" from life in the rest of America. This was written in the early stages of the Reagan campaign against welfare. Nicholas Lemann, later the respected dean of the Columbia School of Journalism and a liberal contributor to *The New Yorker* and *The New York Review of Books*, published two long articles in *The Atlantic* in 1986 announcing that "as apart as all of black life is, ghetto life is a thousand times more so, with a different language, economy, educational system, and social ethic." The difference between the rising black middle class and the underclass was family structure, according to him, and the key sociological fact was out-of-wedlock birth, which was "by far the greatest contributor to the perpetuation of misery of ghetto life." The barrier to upward mobility was "anthropological, not economic."

Both Auletta and Lemann adopted behavioral explanations of poverty disguised by lofty-sounding but inadequately specified cultural causation. Lemann did not trace the dissolution of the black family to slavery, as Daniel Patrick Moynihan, as we shall soon discuss, had done twenty years earlier. Lemann attributed it to the later sharecropper era. But it was a close cousin to Moynihan's idea. Destructive culture lived on unperturbed by economic or technological changes. The poor of this subculture could not become rational participants in a more rewarding economy. "'Underclass' swiftly became the most fashionable term in poverty discourse," wrote one historian.

The left-of-center columnist Pete Hamill, joining in, wrote in 1986 in the *Chicago Tribune*, "Members of the underclass don't share traditional values of work, money, education, home and perhaps even life.... [The underclass] devours every effort aimed at solving its problems, resists solutions both simple and complicated, absorbs more than its share of welfare and other benefits and causes social and political turmoil far and wide." "Dependency," we might say, became among the most fashionable words of the time, to some degree even on the left.

Ironically, in the same years, serious dissident scholars were doing empirical research based on long-term economic data to show that dependency and a subculture of poverty were myths. "Based on over a decade of analysis," writes O'Connor of these scholars' findings in the early 1980s, "poverty and welfare were both 'transitory' conditions, amenable to solution with a better system of income support. This view was considered one of the singular achievements of poverty research, not just because it was an artifact of better, longitudinal data, but also because it put the concept of a permanent culture of poverty to rest."

Since the 1970s, these dissident researchers had favored a universalist cash-oriented approach to reducing poverty because they found so little evidence of dependency. The researchers, among them a young Greg Duncan, found that few of the poor were embedded long-term in poverty. To them, those who argued that an intractable culture of poverty existed were clearly wrong.

But the culturalists and behaviorists began to color too much of the thinking of even first-rate researchers. Mary Jo Bane and David Ellwood of the Harvard Kennedy School found, in a 1983 study, that parsing the data about long-term poor produced a different finding. Such was the environment of the time. Only a minority of the poor were long-termers, but they accounted for a majority of the costs of the existing welfare system that was now being roundly criticized by Reagan, as Nixon had before him. Moreover, while the short-term poor were better educated, white, and married or divorced, the long-term poor were often never-married single mothers, high school dropouts, and black. Adjusting the behavior and work habits of blacks through work requirements was a viable way to reduce long-term poverty, said these liberal analysts. Mary Jo Bane at least warned about too much attention being paid by poverty analysts to family structure, even though her interpretation of the data seemed to support the notion that single mothers were a principal cause of poverty. "Marriage is an important road out of poverty for persons in these families, though, surprisingly perhaps, not as important as work," the wayward liberals wrote in 1983. "Unfortunately," Ellwood and Bane concluded, "the results also open the possibility that dependency may be a serious problem."

As one sociologist put it: "The consequences of 'culture of poverty' arguments have been disastrous. These arguments result in policies that seek to change blacks. If there is equal opportunity, their 'culture of poverty,' in its various guises, contrary to the findings of other progressives, means that African Americans are unable to take advantage of that opportunity."

Behavior was thus seen as the problem, far more so than economics or prejudice. A culture of poverty was to blame, even by many progressives; it was the principal way poverty was created and propagated.

Thus, when Reagan called for large-scale welfare reform in 1986, some moderate and left-of-center economists went along. Ellwood called his own policy "divide and conquer." The short-term poor suffered forgivable economic problems and would be helped differently from the long-term poor, who needed the carrot of work training and the stick of work requirements. Although liberals typically wanted federal job creation programs as part of a requirement for work, as O'Connor notes, they decidedly moved toward the conservative position—while the conservatives gave very little ground. Some liberals who once believed in cash programs and denied that welfare encouraged significant shirking of work had changed their minds. They came to believe that with cash benefit policies, adult poverty remained high, and children suffered as a result.

THE ROLE OF MOYNIHAN

Daniel Patrick Moynihan had given the argument about black culture its forward spin, tapping the latent American appetite for a cultural explanation of black poverty. The former Harvard professor, then a member of Lyndon Johnson's government as undersecretary of labor, wrote about the "tangle of pathology" of the black family in 1965. It was poisonous language.

This "pathology" was the result of "three centuries of injustice [that] have brought about deep-seated structural distortions in the life of the Negro American." The result of this long-standing family dissolution was, supposedly, the rise in unmarried mothers who headed families. In fact, the proportion of female-headed households was just beginning to rise when Moynihan wrote the report; only later would it be a common phenomenon across all ethnic and racial lines in the United States, and indeed in Europe as well. This made Moynihan look prescient, but nonetheless it was hardly likely that the single parentage had to do mostly with family dissolution traceable to slavery or to Lemann's sharecropper era.

In his 1965 report, Moynihan ironically included a chapter arguing that lack of work for black men as well as low wages were major contributors to poverty, a structural and economic rather than a cultural or moral argument. Soon afterward, he was one of the leading advocates for Nixon's cash programs for the poor, and allowances specifically for poor children. And in 1995 he was a leading critic of the new Clinton welfare reform.

But such "structural" factors were hardly mentioned in the controversy his paper caused. His language of pathology couldn't help but engage the consciously or unconsciously racist, as well as long-standing individualist bias. Simply put, what both shocked and appealed to the nation fresh off Great Society legislation was his emphasis on the putative strangeness of the black family and the seeming lack of agency families have to right their own ship. This buttressed the arguments of conservatives who roundly criticized poverty crusades. Moynihan borrowed some of his analysis from the black sociologist E. Franklin Frazier, who was perhaps the first to argue that black family dissolution evolved over a long period beginning with the ravages of slavery but, importantly, was made worse by lack of economic opportunity for men.

Moynihan, however, focused on the purportedly abnormal structure of the black family: matriarchy, and the absence of fathers. Despite his additional claims about the lack of jobs, he emphasized the dominance of a black culture of poverty. He believed that public policy should be directed toward "strengthening the Negro family so as to enable it to raise and support its members as do other families." This typically meant families needed both fathers and mothers.

Simple facts do not support the family dissolution thesis. The historian Herbert Guttman, drawing on Census Bureau data, showed that the majority of blacks from 1750 to 1925 were members of a nuclear family. The twentieth-century data show that the marriage rate of blacks and whites was about equal until well after World War II. According to the Census Bureau, the marriage rate of black women exceeded white women's since 1890, only falling below that of white women in the 1970 census.

Some argued that maternal family structure was in fact a constructive legacy of black life, not a breakdown in its moral fiber. The myopia of most scholars who embraced the Moynihan argument was disappointing and also destructive. There were, fortunately, academic outliers, however. The sociologist Herbert Gans wrote that the matriarchal family "has not yet been proven pathological," citing the studies on maternal networks that had stabilized black families. Dissident anthropologists had long argued the female-headed households among blacks were not a pathology, but a constructive choice. But the "culture of poverty" argument remained dominant. The seemingly progressive appeal of the argument was that you could maintain that black poverty was not an issue of moral character but of the tragic legacy of the past—of slavery—which resulted in fewer marriages, more divorce, unwed mothers, lack of a work ethic, a tendency to crime, and irresponsible black men who had had no constructive role models as children. Progressives who embraced this view could join the popular conservative tidal wave of the 1980s and 1990s.

Nearly three-quarters of all births to black women occur outside marriage. The young black woman who has a child and is head of a household has thus been the easy target of choice, whatever the explanation. The numbers seem to speak for themselves. In turn, nearly half of all black families with children headed by a female without a spouse are poor.

Yet, as noted earlier, the proportion of unmarried mothers has risen for all Americans since the 1960s, in good part a function of cultural change and the greater independence of women who work. Their proportion has risen rapidly in European nations as well. For black women, the proportion roughly flattened out from 1990 forward, well before the welfare reform of 1996.

Aid to Families with Dependent Children, the continuation of the Roosevelt program, expanded sharply in the 1960s when single mothers became eligible. Black women in particular flooded the welfare rolls, having been largely restricted from or unaware of the welfare programs since the 1930s. A powerful welfare rights movement urged them to sign up and increased benefits for all. The bulging payments, especially to blacks, were fodder for conservative policymakers, Ronald Reagan's deceitful "welfare queen" references most notably.

Food stamps were also a focal point of anger and misinformation. According to one survey, they were the most unpopular social policy of the 1980s. Reagan, with the help of Senator Jesse Helms, a constant critic of food stamps, succeeded in cutting the benefits of the program. But it had proven so effective that it was not eliminated, and benefits over time were substantially increased. It is now virtually the only welfare program in America for those who do not have a job, yet even here the "workfare" model crept in. After the 1996 welfare reform, able-bodied adults without dependents (ABAWDs) "can only get SNAP for 3 months in 3 years if they do not meet certain special work requirements. This is called the time limit. To be eligible beyond the time limit, an ABAWD must work at least 80 hours per month, participate in qualifying education and training activities at least 80 hours per month, or comply with a workfare program. Workfare means that ABAWDs can do *unpaid* work through a special state-approved program."

Traditional welfare was radically changed under Bill Clinton. Temporary Aid to Needy Families (TANF), the new American welfare system, now required that recipients work. As a result, it today covers only one-third as many families as it did before. Many poor went without benefits altogether, or took precarious and low-wage jobs. Low-income children in particular became the victims of minimal federal aid. Now the benefits of the three major welfare programs that affect children, other than Medicaid—the EITC, the CTC, and TANF—depended on parents' finding work. And some Republicans are now demanding work requirements for Medicaid.

THE FAILURE OF THE CURRENT AMERICAN
WELFARE SYSTEM: SKEWING AID AWAY
FROM THE MOST NEEDY

A key reason our poverty rate fails to respond adequately, then, is the welfare reform of 1996 that created Temporary Assistance to Needy Families (TANF), sharply reducing cash payments compared to the Aid for Families with Dependent Children (AFDC). Today TANF, which both reduced payments and attached work requirements for recipients, is an insignificant factor in the lives of most poor people and for the most part cannot raise families above the poverty line. Indeed, many who were forced to take jobs are still poor.

As the economist Robert A. Moffitt argues: "On the one hand, the drastic decline in the AFDC-TANF program meant that, while 57 percent of single mother families in private income deep poverty received support from the program in 1983, only 20 percent did by 2004." Social spending shifted away from single mothers and their children to married working couples and the elderly.

Moffitt continues, "On the other hand, the major expansion of the EITC program in the late 1980s and early 1990s provided significant additional support to working single mother families above about $10,000 of annual earnings. And the introduction of the CTC . . . led to additional government support for working single mother families but little or no support to those with low levels of private income. The net result was another redistribution of benefits, in this case from the poorest single mother families to those with higher incomes."

Since he wrote this essay, the CTC has been expanded to $2,000 a year. But his central points remain correct. When Moffitt includes programs such as Social Security and Medicare, which also benefit the poor, he finds that 60 percent of social spending in America goes to those who earn wages that are more than 200 percent of the poverty line.

In sum, there is almost no welfare as we once knew it in America. The strict work requirements and a time limit for recipients of TANF—a maximum of five years—have eliminated many beneficiaries. Demands to search actively for work dissuade applicants, because the search is costly and time-consuming. In 2015, TANF spending came to just 0.54 percent of total federal outlays, so effective had been the campaign against cash welfare in the 1990s. Only 23 percent of poor families received TANF in 2015 compared to 68 percent in 1996, when it started. In fourteen states, only 10 percent of families or fewer received TANF. The benefits adjusted for inflation even when received are far lower than they were in 1996, when TANF passed. And those benefits under the original welfare program, Aid to Families with Dependent Children, had already fallen by 40 percent in real terms in most states between 1970 and 1996.

The current TANF benefits, administered by the states, are no higher than 60 percent of the official poverty line in every state of the union. In thirty-four states, benefits come to less than 30 percent of the poverty line, and in eighteen less than 20 percent. And the states have a variety of ways of keeping the poor off the TANF rolls. In Mississippi, as of 2016, the maximum benefit was $170 a month. In relatively generous California, it was $715 a month, still only roughly 40 percent of the poverty line there. In addition, for all the alleged benefits of workfare requirements, the EITC is more effective in encouraging women to work, raising their payoffs through the carrot of the tax credits rather than the stick of the TANF work mandates. On average, a three-person family who qualify now receives $447 a month in TANF benefits, but in fourteen states the amount comes to less than $300 a month.

For those who cannot get connected to the job market, America is an especially cruel place, and children suffer accordingly. Adding SNAP and TANF together—the only regular income available if parents cannot find work—yields a family budget of more than 75 percent of the official poverty line in only one state (New Hampshire). In roughly twenty states, the two combined programs come to 50 percent or less of the poverty line; in another twenty, no higher than 60 percent.

Ideological battles over the origins of poverty are not an abstraction—they have consequences for the poor, for policy, and for the way that Americans understand who's to blame for poverty. A sweeping study of American media coverage of poverty and its relationship to social policy concluded categorically that Americans have a "negative view of the poor." By contrast, surveys of Europeans find they more closely adhere to a structuralist rather than individualist or behavioral views of poverty. When offered a survey with multiple possible causes for poverty, 70.1 percent of French respondents included "injustice in society" as a cause. So did 87.9 percent of Croatians.

Added to these strong ingrown tendencies in America in the post–World War II period is anti-black racism, of course. Racism was at the heart of welfare reform in the 1990s, I will argue, and it remains one of the major causal factors in the inability of the nation to reduce poverty rates to civilized levels.

CHAPTER 6

RACISM AND POVERTY

We can't understand the inability to deal with child poverty and the related negative connotations of cash welfare to many Americans without recognizing the extent and depth of racism in America. Racism reinforced the distinction between "us" and "them" that is at the center of cultural and individualist ideas about the causes of poverty throughout American history. As Alice O'Connor writes, to repeat, those who argue that individuals or cultures bring poverty on themselves believe in the otherness of the poor.

Legal slavery, followed by the Jim Crow discrimination in the South and simultaneous maltreatment of African Americans in the North, are now widely recognized and decried chapters of American history. But after the partial success of the civil rights legislation of the 1960s, racism reared its head again during the welfare reform debates of the 1980s and 1990s, and police violence toward blacks in recent years.

THE INVISIBILITY OF BLACKS

In the late 1800s, American poverty had a different character than it did in the Great Depression. Farmers and immigrants migrated to the big cities for jobs in manufacturing and related fields. The problem was less unemployment—though that did cyclically recur—than low and sometimes starvation wages in the new mass production industries and, for many, life in unsanitary ghetto-like enclaves. (Average wages were still relatively higher than in the Old World.)

But white, not black, poverty was the main focus of Progressives and social reformers in the late 1800s and early 1900s. Immigrant groups from Germany, Sweden, Italy, Poland, Ireland, and many other countries from across Europe arrived in the United States. Though legally categorized as "white," these European newcomers stimulated a cultural, racialist, and religious prejudice, as Catholics, Jews, and the poor of other nations were seen to have "invaded" America. The Irish were called "Simian-like," to take a vivid example, sketched in the periodicals as "Celtic ape-men with sloping foreheads and monstrous appearances."

In the Great Depression, poverty ran deep and spread widely across urban and rural America, encompassing both whites and blacks. Unemployment rose to more than 30 percent of the population. As Harrington wrote, poverty was "the decisive social experience" of the time. According to today's poverty line, adjusted for inflation, one-half to two-thirds of the nation were poor in those years.

The image of poverty during the 1930s was influenced by the widely distributed Dorothea Lange photographs of poor *white* farmers in the drought-ridden Plains. John Steinbeck's *The Grapes of Wrath*, published in 1939, captured the public imagination as his starving Okie and Arkie families, and those from Kansas, Missouri, and elsewhere, left for the promise of a better life. In the big cities, the iconic image of poverty was the white man selling apples. Lange photographed the white poor in San Francisco in their makeshift residences.

Little attention was given by the media, social reformers, or policymakers to the black poor, most of whom had been struggling since emancipation. (There was no category yet for Hispanics in the federal statistics.) Lange photographed only a handful of black workers in rural America during the Depression. A frequently cited book on 1930s poverty, Isaac Max Rubinow's 638-page *The Quest for Security*, mentioned black poverty just once: "Predictions were made of the ultimate disappearance of the negro in America because of that high mortality rate, but the improvement of the economic and educational status of the negro during the last twenty years has reduced the death rate."

THE VISIBILITY OF BLACKS

The image of poverty did not seriously change during the migration of blacks to the North in the 1940s and 1950s, as they searched for manufacturing and

other good jobs, even though the black population of
major cities soared. But in the 1950s, black protests for
civil rights started to spread. The 1954 Supreme Court
decision *Brown v. Board of Education,* which required
Topeka, Kansas, public schools to be integrated, was a
major victory against institutional prejudice. Resistance
remained. Orval Faubus, the governor of Arkansas,
made headlines by refusing nine black children entry
into a public school in Little Rock. The Republican
president Eisenhower sent troops to open the schools.

In 1955, the civil rights veteran activist Rosa Parks
refused to cede her seat in the black section of the bus in
Montgomery, Alabama, inspiring a bus boycott locally
and in other cities. (She had predecessors who had done
the same.) Martin Luther King Jr. was among the early
organizers. In 1962, the year Harrington published *The
Other America,* the black student James Meredith reg-
istered for the all-white University of Mississippi and
captured the media's attention. In 1963, King led his
massive March on Washington for civil rights and jobs.
Johnson's Civil Rights Act of 1964, Voting Rights Act
of 1965, and Fair Housing Act of 1968 were a turning
point for the federal government—Johnson knew when
he signed them that he would lose critical Democratic
support in the South. Presidents Kennedy and Johnson both signed executive orders on "affirmative action,"
Kennedy in 1961. But Kennedy's was comparatively
tepid.

Black riots exploded in Harlem and Newark in
1964, spread to Watts in Los Angeles, and then to
Detroit and other major cities. "In 1966, the country

saw 43 race riots; in 1967, 164 riots left 83 people dead," writes the policy analyst Richard Kahlenberg. In the meantime, crime rates were rising in big cities, and new political fault lines emerged. "For several decades, Americans ha[d] voted basically along the lines of property," the commentators Richard Scammon and Ben Wattenberg wrote in 1970. "Suddenly, sometime in the late 1960s, 'crime,' and 'race' and 'lawlessness' and 'civil rights' became the most important domestic issues in America."

Though he had organized economic protests before, King's Poor People's Campaign of 1968 was a dramatic formal demand for economic equality—for all poor Americans, including blacks. King organized the building of a famed tent city on the Washington Mall. The movement proposed a guaranteed minimum income, housing supports, and a commitment to full-employment policies. The sit-in collapsed after King's assassination in the spring of 1968.

Robert Kennedy, who had seen starvation close up in the Deep South, was murdered shortly after King. There was wrenching dissension among Democrats over the Vietnam War and poverty programs, and the televised police riots at the Democratic convention in Chicago in the summer of 1968 stunned the nation. Black Power became the emblem of some young black men and women who were demanding recognition in white America.

As blacks pressed their demands in the nonviolent demonstrations of King and the more disruptive riots (though many felt threatened by King's nonviolent marches as well), working-class Democrats voted in large numbers for Republicans. George Wallace, the racist firebrand from Alabama, got support from white working-class voters in the North when he ran for president in 1968. Richard Nixon's so-called Southern Strategy during his presidential run that year, in which crime was a major theme, was an attempt to win white working-class Democrats to the Republican side. As one of its architects, Kevin Phillips, wrote, "The more Negroes who register as Democrats in the South, the sooner the Negrophobe whites will quit the Democrats and become Republicans."

In this period, the poverty rate fell sharply, but then flattened out. As black visibility in America grew, a voluble conservative punditry successfully argued that the War on Poverty had failed. It hadn't, as we've seen, but the growing number of black welfare recipients in the 1960s was a lightning rod for white anger. Welfare easily aggravated the existing individualist and racist attitudes of the nation.

MISUNDERSTANDING WHO IS POOR

Blacks are not the dominant race or ethnicity among the poor in America, but according to surveys, as we shall see, most Americans think they are. There are 16.9 million poor whites, roughly double the number of poor blacks and 60 percent more than poor Hispanics. Forty-two percent of the poor are white, 29 percent are Hispanic, and 23 percent are black. A far higher percentage of people of color, however, are poor than are whites.

Nearly one-third of black children are poor, one-

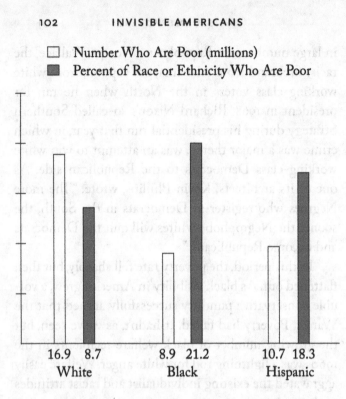

□ Number Who Are Poor (millions)
■ Percent of Race or Ethnicity Who Are Poor

16.9 8.7   8.9 21.2   10.7 18.3
  White   Black   Hispanic

Source: Jessica L. Semega, Kayla R. Fontenot, and Melissa A. Kollar, *Income and Poverty in the United States: 2017* (Washington, DC: United States Census Bureau, 2018), 12.

fourth of Hispanic kids, and one-tenth of white youth. Still, the number of poor white children exceeds 4 million and the number of poor black children comes to about 3 million. The number of poor Hispanic children exceeds 4.5 million, because Latino families typically have more children.

Eight percent of all children live in families whose incomes are half the official poverty line—deep poverty.

About 2.1 million of these are children under age five. About 15 percent of black children and 10 percent of Hispanic children live in deep poverty.

Whites benefit far more from government social programs for low-income people than do either blacks or Hispanics—even when the latter two groups of color are combined. In 2010, whites made up 64 percent of the population but received 69 percent of social benefits. Hispanics received only 12 percent of government benefits, though they made up 16 percent of the population. Included in this calculation are benefits from Social Security, Medicare, Medicaid, food stamps, TANF, and housing assistance, and major tax credits such as the Earned Income Tax Credit and the Child Tax Credit.

Conversely, when benefits are cut, they have a greater impact on white Americans than on those of color—a fact to which the electorate seems oblivious.

DEPENDENCY

One indication of racial misconceptions—and racism itself—is that, according to surveys, Americans overestimate by a wide margin the number of blacks who are officially poor. One survey asked, "Of all the people who are poor in this country, are more of them black or are more of them white?" Fifty-five percent of Americans in the 1990s answered "black" and 24 percent "white," at a time when demands for cutting welfare benefits reached their height. To the question "What percent[age] of all the poor people in this country would you say are black?" the typical (median) person answered 50 percent. The actual proportion is about half that.

Ronald Reagan's race-baiting in the 1970s and 1980s had had a lasting impact. To him, as with others, welfare was the cause, not the cure, of poverty. It promoted laziness and dependency. His welfare queen anecdotes were atrocious. The black woman Reagan cited as a welfare queen in his first presidential campaign in 1976 did exist—but Reagan wildly exaggerated her cheating, his "research" based on tabloid media reports.

"She has eighty names," he said, "thirty addresses, twelve Social Security cards, and is collecting veterans benefits on four non-existing deceased husbands." He went on, "She's collecting Social Security on her cards. She's got Medicaid, getting food stamps, and she is collecting welfare under each of her names. Her tax-free cash income alone is over $150,000."

The woman's name was Linda Taylor. She was indeed claiming more benefits than legally allowed, but contrary to Reagan's claims—which he made repeatedly during the New Hampshire primary in 1976—she had not twelve but four Social Security cards. The government found that she made only $8,000, not twenty times that. The median household income in the United States was $12,690 at the time.

In another case, Reagan told his audiences at town meetings and in formal speeches that there was a low-income housing project in Harlem with a swimming pool and a gym, offering apartments with eleven-foot ceilings, for $113 a month. But only 15 percent of the apartments had such ceilings, and they came with rents of $450 a month—and no apartments in the building cost less than $300 a month for welfare recipients. The pool was for community use, for the 200,000 or so black, Puerto Rican, and other immigrant Americans in the neighborhood.

Reagan also claimed that as governor he removed twice as many recipients from the California welfare rolls as was the case. He often exaggerated by a multiple the cost of federal welfare—the Aid for Families with Dependent Children program, which was small—by including the far greater expenditures for Social Security and Medicare in the number. AFDC spending came to 0.6 percent of GDP in the 1980s. If food stamps were included, the budget came to roughly 1 percent.

He denied that the War on Poverty was of any benefit. Reagan's masterpiece was his often-made claim, repeated in his 1988 State of the Union address, that "the federal government fought a War on Poverty, and poverty won." How had this idea become "common sense" in the 1980s?

Conservative scholars and journalists in the wake of the War on Poverty often wrote scathingly, and irresponsibly, about the behavioral causes of poverty. The first major best seller along these lines was *Wealth and Poverty*, by George Gilder. It was an ideological screed, published in 1981, just when Ronald Reagan took office as president, on the benefits of supply-side economics.

The free market would, once unencumbered, produce widespread prosperity, Gilder argued. If low taxes produced large federal budget deficits, as they did under Reagan (and are doing under Donald Trump), rapid

economic growth would soon eliminate them. Welfare
policies were a distortion that disrupted the purity of
the market and inhibited growth. They were allegedly
wasted funds that contributed nothing to productivity—
a deadweight loss. John Maynard Keynes, the economist upon whose work the late New Deal and postwar
order rested, would have argued that, to the contrary,
such policies help bolster aggregate demand for goods
and services and therefore more growth.

The anti-welfare ideologues of course generally
believed welfare programs themselves created more
demand for welfare as recipients shirked work and
became dependent. If welfare was abandoned, poverty
would be minimized, they argued. Gilder's book offered
no statistical evidence in support of this view, which,
far from hindering its popularity, no doubt contributed
to it.

Still more influential was the best seller *Losing
Ground*, by the political scientist and arch-reactionary
theorist of race Charles Murray. Published in 1984,
it was heavy with statistics. The theme was that rising welfare rolls, higher rates of female-headed black
households and teenage mothers, and quite a few other
alleged behavioral maladies were the consequences of
welfare benefits, particularly AFDC and food stamps.
After being discarded by careful analysts in the 1970s
and early 1980s as insupportable because long-term
welfare recipients were simply too few, this theory of
dependency became the new "truth" of the 1980s and
1990s and fit longstanding American attitudes about
the poor and blacks like a glove.

The array of statistics in Murray's book misled many a reader. One example was the assertion that the rising value of welfare and SNAP stamps made it possible to stop working—indeed, Murray argued the value of welfare and food stamps exceeded the wage that could be earned by many. He did not take into account the fact that the value of the government programs adjusted for inflation began to decline sharply by 1972 (the beginning of a decade of rapid inflation). The states, which administered the programs, did not raise benefits along with the soaring prices. As wages rose with inflation, they were actually now unambiguously higher than welfare benefits, which in Murray's thinking meant that the poor would just get jobs.

The determination of scholars like Murray, and their all-important support from the right-wing foundations and donors that paid handsome salaries to their fellows and analysts, was a major reason why American poverty policy has been inadequate. Now this onslaught would turn the tables completely.

THE WELFARE REFORM
THAT RACISM MADE POSSIBLE

In 1994 Murray published *The Bell Curve* with the psychologist Richard Herrnstein. Another best seller, the book argued, among other things, and most memorably, that blacks had innately inferior IQs. Again, distortionary tricks were played on readers. Its claims were easily discredited by scholars.

To take an important example of Murray and Herrnstein's misleading logic, black IQs in America were lower than white IQs, which many scholars had accurately traced to poor education, child poverty, and uneducated parents, as well as skewed questions and testing methodology. But the authors wanted to show that these low IQs were hereditary. One somersault in their reasoning was that the IQs of African Americans rose over the decades as they intermarried with whites. Their "proof" was that Africans' IQs in Africa, where intermarriage with whites was rare, were lower than black IQs in America. Statisticians pointed out that accurately measuring IQs in Africa was impossible, and that the authors' assertions were indefensible. But dissenters, writing, "It has been more difficult to assemble data on the score of the average African black than one would expect," did not give Murray and Herrnstein any pause.

In 2000, Murray wrote that one could not imagine a politician admitting that a large proportion of poor people are poor because they are just inherently, biologically lazy. Murray went on, "You cannot imagine it because that kind of thing cannot be said. And yet this unimaginable statement merely implies that when we know the complete genetic story, it will turn out that the population below the poverty line in the United States has a configuration of the relevant genetic makeup that is significantly different from the configuration of the population above the poverty line. This is not unimaginable. It is almost certainly true."

To the contrary, it was untrue and has to this

day not been proved. Murray and Herrnstein, contrary to the image they cultivated, did little original research, taking their statistical conclusions from other right-wing scholars, merely adding an extra serving of invective. But they successfully gave false statistical credibility to long-held racial stereotypes. *The Bell Curve* was constantly cited during the 1990s welfare reform discourse—its hard racialism gave cover to Gingrich and Clinton's more sensible-seeming attacks on social programs. But Murray and Herrnstein's book did have vocal supporters in high places. Chester E. Finn Jr., once the assistant secretary of education in the Reagan administration, effused, "Even if only half or one quarter of this book endures the assault, its implications will be as profound for the beginning of the new century as Michael Harrington's discovery of 'the other America' was for the final part of the old."

MEASURING RACISM

In 1999, the political scientist Martin Gilens published a study of the racial attitudes of whites and blacks over these years called *Why Americans Hate Welfare*. Analyzing the many opinion surveys he had gathered, Gilens reported that Americans supported many social programs such as job training and the Earned Income Tax Credit, but they were overwhelmingly opposed to welfare, which was a cash distribution with few conditions. Many were also decidedly opposed to food stamps—and federal policy began to change: the job search requirement for some food stamp enrollees was instituted in 1977, for example. Although the percentage of families receiving AFDC tripled in the ten years up to 1975, total federal spending for the program had flattened out as a percentage of GDP well before the welfare reform of 1996. Average monthly SNAP benefits in the mid-1990s were only $70 per person.

These facts did not mitigate American antagonism. In the 1990s, Gilens reported, 60 to 70 percent believed America was spending too much on welfare, and some 43 percent believed spending on food stamps should be cut. Harking back to these glory days for the American right, Republicans have recently proposed another sharp increase in work requirements for food stamps.

Strong indications of bias against blacks turned up in Gilens's surveys. "I find that racial attitudes have a profound impact on opposition to welfare, both directly and by shaping perceptions of the deservingness of welfare recipients," he concluded. "Whites' attitudes toward poverty and welfare are dominated by their beliefs about blacks."

THE FACE OF POVERTY

The face of poverty in America finally became a black one in the 1960s as the long historical prejudice against the poor was reinforced by racism. Gilens attributes much of this extreme overestimate to the way poverty was illustrated in print and television media by black people. He analyzed the media representation of the poor over the preceding forty-five years in *Time*,

Newsweek, and *U.S. News & World Report,* as well as in network television news coverage. After being ignored for so long, poor blacks suddenly became the primary focus of media stories on poverty in the 1960s.

This coincided with the racial unrest and widespread riots. But as urban riots subsided and the country's attention turned toward Vietnam, Watergate, and the economic problems of the 1970s, the racial portrayal of the poor in news coverage did not return to the predominantly white images of the 1950s and early 1960s. Instead, the black representation of the poor in images of poverty stayed high, fluctuating somewhat with the state of the economy.

Gilens found that there were high numbers of blacks illustrating poverty stories in 1972 and 1973 when welfare rolls expanded and simultaneously fewer whites were threatened by poverty in a strong economy. But, as he puts it, there was a moderate "whitening of poverty images" when the economy slid into recession in 1974 and 1975, and again in 1982 and 1983, when more of the white population was threatened by poverty.

Overall, blacks were the focus of 57 percent of stories about poverty in the media he examined between 1967 and 1992—twice the ratio of poor blacks in the population. When the welfare population grew most rapidly in 1972 and 1973, blacks were the focus of 70 percent of the media stories about poverty.

There are many studies of how influential media representation can be. In one experiment, researchers showed two television news stories about an unemployed person to white study participants. In one segment, the unemployed person was black, and in the other segment, he was white. Seventy-one percent of those who viewed the clip featuring an unemployed white worker said that unemployment was one of the three most important issues in the nation. Only 53 percent who watched a story about a black unemployed worker thought so.

Too many whites believe blacks do not work hard and therefore do not deserve, nor will they make constructive use of, unconditional cash benefits. In one study, of the 55 percent of respondents who believed most welfare recipients are black, "sixty-three percent said that 'lack of effort on their own part' is most often to blame when people are on welfare, while only 26 percent blamed 'circumstances beyond their control.' But among respondents who knew most welfare recipients are white, 50 percent blamed circumstances and only 40 percent attributed the problem to a lack of effort."

Some analysts postulated that once welfare was reformed and made work-based, anger would subside, and Americans would be less prejudiced toward welfare recipients and blacks in general. An example often cited by such analysts was the passage of CHIP, insurance for children above the poverty line, in 1997. But passing this legislation was difficult, led by Senators Ted Kennedy and Orrin Hatch, a notable, rare, and bitterly fought bipartisan victory.

The scholar Bas van Doorn updated Martin Gilens's findings from the welfare reform era of the 1990s in a 2015 research study to test the thesis that the reforms of the 1990s would assuage white antagonism. In the 2000s, antagonism toward welfare and food stamps fell from the unusually steep highs of the 1990s, but they hovered at the same high levels of the 1980s when Reagan was president and Gilder and Murray were stoking racial fury. Van Doorn also found that blacks continued to be overrepresented in media stories on poverty in general.

Affirmative action, begun symbolically by Kennedy and pursued with some seriousness by Johnson, seems to be widely regarded by most Americans as a gift intended to compensate for a historical wrong. But affirmative action for blacks—or the still more controversial cash reparations for slavery—are not designed to give contemporary blacks a monetary bonus because their ancestors were harmed, or to punish whites for slavery or racism. They are meant to compensate for the reality that the effects of racist policies persist in contemporary form.

The legal exclusion of blacks from so many opportunities to advance was built into the American way of life. As Richard Rothstein summarizes in his eye-opening 2017 book, *The Color of Law*, government policies have created an unlevel playing field for black citizens since Reconstruction. After federal troops no longer protected emancipated blacks in the South in 1877, they were deprived of their votes by state governments and soon subjected to sharecropping on former slaveholders' lands. Jim Crow laws were adopted to segregate blacks in public places, including schools, for the next century.

The historian and political scientist Ira Katznelson

documented in his classic book *When Affirmative Action Was White* how blacks were intentionally restricted from the benefits of Roosevelt's New Deal, including Social Security. Blacks were deprived of the full benefits of the otherwise magnanimous and effective GI Bill of Rights. Rothstein describes how federal and state governments for the most part refused to subsidize mortgages for blacks. Nor did government prevent segregation by residential real estate developers and racial redlining by private banks. Levittown, the pioneering suburb on Long Island, prohibited sales to blacks, as did other communities. I went to Levittown public schools, and I never really knew a black person until I was in college.

With redlining and suburban segregation, blacks could not benefit from the real estate asset boom since the 1960s that provided a substantial future net worth for whites. Black schools are functionally segregated today and generally poorly financed, as poverty is increasingly centralized in poor neighborhoods. Declining real wages for lower-income Americans over thirty years are critical to the story of poverty—and in particular black poverty.

CHAPTER 7

HARDSHIP AND POVERTY

The mismeasurement of poverty in America is deliberate. That fact is not lost on government experts. As Denton Vaughan, a respected Social Security analyst, has put it: "Updating the statistical measure of poverty would tend to change our view of the size of the poverty population and thus affect our sense of the possible claim which poverty reduction, as a policy goal, has on national resources. As there are very powerful forces arrayed on each side of the poverty debate, the resulting political sensitivity of the poverty issue has very obviously contributed to the difficulty of modifying the current measure."

What would it take to measure poverty fairly in America?

The problems of the current measures of poverty—official and supplemental—are manifold. For example, a simple income poverty line is inadequate in telling us how children live in families making less than that line. Even if we measured poverty more accurately, we would still need to know more about how far below the poverty line most poor children fall. While the Census

Bureau regularly reports the number of children in deep poverty, this tells us precious little. In 2017, 8 percent of children—almost 6 million, based on the OPM—lived in families below half of the poverty line.

Under the supplemental measure, tax credits and benefits such as SNAP, school lunches, and housing benefits raise some very poor children out of deep poverty, but they typically remain under the poverty line even so, making them subject to serious disadvantages. Only some 4.8 percent of children are in deep poverty under the SPM, a fact much applauded without sufficiently considering that so many children are poor according to a measure that is too low.

Earlier, we looked at a handful of examples of how children live in poverty. Now we will more comprehensively examine the daunting *hardship* poor children must bear in order to give a fuller picture of living in poverty.

THE POVERTY GAP

The poverty gap is a useful measure, which compares the income of the poor child at the median of all poor children, or the typical poor child—as a reminder, the middle of the pack—to the country's poverty line. UNICEF, the United Nations organization dedicated to child welfare, uses a relative poverty measure based on median family incomes to compare child poverty by nation. The agency found in 2012 that the typical (median) poor child in America has an annual income 37.5 percent below the poverty line. A typical poor child in France is only 15 percent below the poverty line. In Finland, the typical child in poverty is only 11 percent below the poor line. Clearly, a much higher proportion of poor American children are living on incomes well below the poverty line compared to the rest of our peers. If the poverty line is a subsistence level, many children are living in destitution.

There may have been 1.5 million families whose members live on $2 a day before counting SNAP, in 2016. Other scholars argue that SNAP must be counted, which would reduce the number at so low a level of poverty. The controversy can get technical, but SNAP is not the equivalent of cash, and as discussed, these families still mostly live in deep poverty. Based on the pre-SNAP computation, nearly half of those living on $2 a day were white, and a third of the families were headed by couples.

What solutions to this crisis is the federal government offering today? Trump economists wanted to adapt TANF-style work requirements to Medicaid and SNAP, claiming too many shirk work. In fact, programs premised on work requirements have exacerbated poverty. The policy analysts Arloc Sherman and Danilo Trisi have definitively shown that the number of children in deep poverty—living below half the official poverty line—increased since TANF was passed. As Sherman and Trisi write, "If the safety net had remained as effective at keeping families out of deep poverty in 2005 as in 1995, 1.2 million children would have been below half the poverty line in 2005; instead, 2.2 million were (based on an adjusted estimate of the poverty rate)."

In 1995, the original cash welfare program AFDC

raised 61 percent of children above deep poverty. Ten years later, TANF raised only 22 percent out of that abyss. SNAP, whose benefits were reduced (and eliminated for most legal immigrants, a policy reversed in 2002) with welfare reform in 1996, kept 62 percent of children out of deep poverty in 1995 compared to only 42 percent in 2005.

Studies show that residual damage results in families who earn above the official poverty line. One such study found that family incomes up to even two times government poverty lines have a significant negative impact on the future wages of children. The effect diminishes as the income gets higher.

Children who lived in families earning roughly $75,000 a year for a family of four show increased income as adults. As I said earlier, my ideal poverty line would be a demarcation above which little damage is done to children, or conversely below which damage begins to be done.

Most telling, there is overwhelming evidence that shows damage to children who live *well* above the poverty line. A study of families with children in New York City is especially alarming and adds weight to the argument for a higher poverty line. According to this study, significant material hardship, such as difficulty paying utility bills, food insecurity, housing instability, and medical problems, is borne by families whose incomes are well above the poverty line. Nearly three out of four low-income New Yorkers earning up to double the poverty line reported one or more such hardships in 2011.

Income-to-Needs Ratio During Childhood	Effect on Adult Income
Below .50 of the poverty line	-.728*
0.5-1.0	-.495*
1.0-1.5	-.342*
1.5-2.0	-.181*
2.0-2.5	-.066
2.5-3.0	(omitted category)
3.0-4.0	+.072
4.0-5.0	+.081
5.0 up	+.136

Source: "TABLE 15.3 / Childhood Predictors of Adults' Log Total Family Income-to-Needs Ratio under Alternative Family Income Specifications, Full Sample," Mary Corcoran and Terry Adams, "Race, Sex, and the Intergenerational Transmission of Poverty," in Greg J. Duncan and Jeanne Brooks-Gunn, eds., *Consequences of Growing Up Poor* (New York: Russell Sage Foundation, 1999), 472.

MATERIAL DEPRIVATION

Some prominent scholars once rejected the relationship between poverty and material deprivation, seeing poverty as a mere "indicator" of diminished well-being, but most now accept it. Poverty itself serves as an index of those hardships.

A survey of material deprivation endured by families in highly developed nations that are members of the Organization for Economic Co-operation and Development (OECD), including the United States, was compiled by scholars in the early 2000s. Individuals were asked about food availability, paying heat and utility bills, keeping up with mortgage payments, overcrowded housing, and how difficult in general it was to make ends meet. The United States was near the bottom of the pack according to these material measures, more or less matching its international ranking on poverty overall.

What are these material deprivations in poor children's lives?

HUNGER

About one in six children in America are not sure where their next meal will come from—as noted earlier, they are what the Agriculture Department defines as food insecure. In 2015, 43.5 percent of children living below the official poverty line experienced such food insecurity. As incomes rise above the poverty line, a large if lesser proportion of families still remain food insecure. Of those whose family incomes are up to 1.3 times the official poverty line, for example, some 19.6 percent have low food security. Even including family incomes as high as 1.85 times the poverty line, 18.2 percent have low food security. Still another reason for establishing a higher poverty line.

About 1 percent of all families with children under eighteen have very low food security—the measure of outright hunger in America, according to the Agriculture Department. Among the poor, about twice that proportion have very low food security. "Household food insecurity has insidious effects on the health and development of young children," writes one specialist, "including increased hospitalizations, poor health, iron deficiency, developmental risk and behavior problems, primarily aggression, anxiety, depression, and attention deficit disorder."

NEUROLOGICAL DAMAGE

The most disturbing finding in the last twenty years of intensive research into the consequences of child poverty is the potential impact of poverty on the neurology of the brain. By and large, when advocates for children discuss ways to ameliorate the consequences of child poverty, they focus on "early interventions" such as home visiting. That's because poor families are often materially unable to provide an educational environment. Children know far fewer words when they grow up in poverty; they have little access to books, nor are they read to. In a pathbreaking 1997 study, Jeanne Brooks-Gunn (a developmental psychologist) and Greg Duncan (an economist) showed, among other things, that poor children were 1.3 times more likely to have a learning disability, and two times as likely to repeat grades.

In a comparison between children in deep poverty (half the poverty line) and those between one and a half and two times the poverty line, the researchers found that IQ was reduced between 6 and 13 percentage points on average for the deep poverty group. The difference can mean, for example, being placed in a special education class.

Brooks-Gunn and Duncan explored the studies of poor children's health, in particular low birth weight and infant mortality, which can be markers of significant health problems in the future. America's high proportion of low-birth-weight babies and infant mortality has long been a disgraceful mark on its record of care for children. Low-birth-weight babies have more learning disabilities, do less well on intelligence tests as they grow older, and repeat grades more frequently. They are also more prone to death in infancy. Such consequences are also generally true for children with stunted growth—that is, they are significantly shorter than their peers. Stunting is caused by nutritional deprivation, and the incidence of stunting is significantly higher among poor children than non-poor children. These same deprived children had lower achievement scores and other indications of damage.

Research about the neurological impact of poverty has reinforced the urgency of very early intervention, including prenatal programs. The neurological research is built on a hypothesis about what researchers now call toxic stress. Stress is one of the pathways scholars have researched in an attempt to establish how poverty damages children. Some stress can be constructive, because it helps develop responses and defenses to the normal activities of life. But for poor children in particular, stress can be so persistent, with hormones released at such excessive rates, that it may do significant damage. Such toxic stress among the poor can take the form of "recurrent physical and/or emotional abuse, chronic neglect, severe maternal depression, parental substance abuse, and family violence," as two scholars put it. It can also come from the anxiety and uncertainty of poverty itself. "Toxic stress refers to strong, frequent, and or prolonged activation of the body's stress-response systems in the absence of the buffering protection of stable adult support," writes one researcher. The impact can also affect infants in the womb due to prenatal stress from substance abuse or a mother's depression.

Startlingly, it has been found that toxic stress disrupts the development of "brain architecture, adversely affects other organs, and leads to stress management systems that establish relatively lower thresholds for responsiveness that persist throughout life, thereby increasing the risk of stress-related disease or disorders as well as cognitive impairment well into the adult years."

Other research suggests the reduced "gray matter"

in the cortex accounted for 15 to 20 percent of lower achievement levels for poor children. A study of six-to-nine-month-old infants found lower electrical activity in the frontal cortex of poor children compared to higher-income infants. There was also measurable damage for children living at 150 percent of the poverty line.

But emotional and cognitive support from parents or health professionals can ameliorate or even reverse the brain damage. A National Institutes of Health study based on MRIs of about three hundred children showed "reduced growth trajectories for total, frontal, and parietal gray matter volumes that were most pronounced for children in poverty." The study also found that higher levels of parental educational attainment, and by implication income, were associated with more "gray matter" in children. Associations of pediatricians are now actively developing methodologies and protocols for their members to detect and address signs of toxic stress in their young, poor patients. The authors of the MRI study emphasized the social importance of preventing or ameliorating poverty-related adversity early in children's lives, drawing on an extensive body of literature that shows the plasticity of the brain's executive functions and development in response to early intervention.

Both social scientists and pediatricians now argue that poverty reduction is an essential part of healthcare for the nation's poor—to ensure the healthy functioning of the brain. As the pioneering researcher in this field, Jack Shonkoff, concludes, "The lifelong costs of childhood toxic stress are enormous." It is also likely that more income and learning, even later in childhood, can mitigate or reverse the brain damage of early toxic stress. Research is now under way on this issue.

THE IMPACT ON CHILDREN: EDUCATION

Low-income children increasingly go to schools predominantly attended by low-income classmates. These schools are usually underfunded because they are largely supported by local taxes. One study finds that states spend 15 percent less on schools in their poorest districts. This is old-fashioned segregation.

Today, more than 50 percent of students in public schools in America are from low-income families, according to the Southern Education Foundation, and the trend has sharply worsened since 1995. Again, there is racial imbalance. Black students attend these high-poverty schools in significantly greater numbers than do whites.

The proportion of low-income students in public high schools was 33 percent in 1995 and 38 percent in 2000. It jumped to more than 50 percent after the Great Recession that officially ended in 2009, and has remained at that high level.

A staggering 24 percent of American public school students attend a "high-poverty school," where 75 percent of students are from low-income households. Only 8 percent of white students do—but 45 percent of Hispanic students attended high-poverty schools, as did 45 percent of black students, 37 percent of American Indian and Alaska Native students, and 25 percent of Pacific Islander students. Students of color are far more likely to attend school with a preponderance of other low-income, working-class students.

About 40 percent of all low-income children attend high-poverty schools. Only 6 percent of American public school students (or about one out of sixteen) attend low-poverty schools, defined as schools where no more than 25 percent of students are low-income.

This is a measure of the extent of segregation along income lines as well as along racial lines. While this is partly a question of geographic diversity, it is essentially a question of unequal resources. As the Urban Institute writes, "The children who need the most are concentrated in schools least likely to have the resources to meet those needs." Moreover, "in some metropolitan areas, the racial concentration of school poverty is so severe that black and white students effectively attend two different school systems: one for middle- and upper-middle-income white students, and the other for poor students and students of color."

"Low-income" as defined in these studies refers to those who live in households that earn 1.85 times or less than the official poverty measure, the eligibility threshold for the federal school lunch program. The 1.85 multiple is the cutoff for qualification for the school lunch program, and thus provides a good estimate of the number of low-income children in schools. That factor of 1.85 yields a more accurate poverty line of $39,460 for a single-parent family with two children.

The growth in the number of low-income students in public schools has been concentrated in the South, but has also occurred in central cities in the North and Midwest. The ten poorest public school districts in 2012 included Muskegon Heights, Michigan; Barbourville, Kentucky; Yazoo City, Mississippi; New Boston, Ohio; and San Perlita, Texas. Just as poor children have become more segregated from the rest of American life, poverty has taken root in almost every corner of the country.

The deck remains tragically stacked against poor children, particularly poor children of color. One million children were not counted in the last national census in 2010; about 400,000 of these uncounted children were Latino. Thus, poor and working-class communities are short-changed of government aid. The size of many programs is determined by the census. These include Medicaid, CHIP, SNAP, WIC, school lunches, and Head Start.

Information is the beginning of decent government in a democracy. But antipoverty policy has no such foundation. If the truer number of struggling Americans were known, the nation might be more generous and wiser in its antipoverty policies, including those that address child poverty.

The most effective way to remedy this injustice to the poor is to redefine the poverty line in realistic rather than political terms.

CHANGING THE POVERTY MEASUREMENT

A humane and caring nation would measure poverty in several ways simultaneously: separate measures to describe what's materially necessary, what's necessary to participate fully in society, and a measure of deprivation relative to the rest of society.

Peter Townsend wrote that there are three kinds of poverty lines. There is an absolute poverty line like America's. In this case, it is set to a subsistence level of living, a survival line. Second, there is a basic needs poverty line, based on a budget empirically observed, regarding what specific goods and services the poor need. The Nobel Prize winner Amartya Sen believes the nation needs such an absolute poverty budget with specified minimum needs: adequate food, housing, healthcare, entertainment, education, and home enrichment. He believes these are needed to provide people with the necessary "capabilities," the concept he and his co-authors developed, to lead a full life. By contrast, the U.S. Agriculture Department produces a "thrifty" budget for food, but it is inadequate by almost any standard, assuming, for example, that the poor must cook nearly everything at home.

The third kind of poverty line would be a true measure of relative deprivation, compared to norms in society. It would measure the tools and services needed to grow and thrive in a changing society—and it would measure where the poor stand compared to others in society. Relative deprivation, Townsend argues, is a significant hardship in itself.

His definition of relative deprivation is as good as we have. He wrote, "Individuals, families, and groups in the population can be said to be in poverty when they lack the resources to obtain the type of diet, participate in the activities, and have the living conditions and the amenities which are customary, or at least widely encouraged or approved, in the societies to which they belong. Their resources are so seriously below those commanded by the average family that they are in effect excluded from the ordinary living patterns, customs, and activities."

But neither Sen nor Townsend believes that a relative measure of poverty based on a percentage of median incomes is adequate, as is common in Europe. Both want more detailed listings of needs, not simply a percentage of income level.

A list of categories of deprivations may include, according to a Townsend disciple, their "household possessions, their housing, their neighborhoods, their community services and their ability to make ends meet." Such an analysis today can focus on lack of goods such as cell phones, computers, access to the web, and adequate public education. Other more conventional measures cited by analysts include whether a family cannot pay the rent or afford to go to the dentist, or whether they have leaks in the roof or exposed wires in the house. Sen's lists of such needs—his *capabilities*, as he called them—included "being alive," "moving about freely," "being well-nourished," "being in good health," "having self respect and respect of others," "being well-sheltered," and "taking part in the life of the community."

Other measures of deprivation can be even more sophisticated. For example, the stages of fulfillment of the noted psychologist Abraham Maslow, writing during World War II, can be considered a set of achievable dimensions that all should be able to pursue if not fully attain. These are physical survival needs, safety needs, social and emotional needs, esteem, and what Maslow calls self-actualization.

The goals of Townsend and Sen throw open a horizon of new vistas for poverty policy. But we could start with a relative poverty line set at 50 percent of median family income. This would still be less than what most of Europe uses to define low income families, but it would nevertheless be a way to keep up with the elasticity of poverty, as demands change in a more prosperous economy. A relative poverty measure, though imperfect, would alleviate many material deprivations and would, for the first time, make the permanent social inclusion of the poor in American prosperity a goal of federal policy. The definition of who is poor would be more properly adjusted as the standard of living rises. The OPM and SPM could also be substantially raised to start again at 50 percent of median incomes, the level the OPM reached when it was first implemented in the 1960s. My own idealistic view, to repeat, is that research could advance to a point where we know at what level child poverty does measurable damage. This would be the new poverty threshold.

Policymakers to a degree recognize the inadequacies of the OPM and even the SPM. Medicaid payments are, thankfully, awarded to those up to 130 percent of the official poverty line. As noted, the federal school lunch program, and many state supplemental programs, are provided to children who live in families that earn up to 185 percent of the poverty line. CHIP, the insurance program for children, has a cutoff line well above the official measure. SNAP is available up to 130 percent of the poverty line. In New York City, all public school students are entitled to government financed lunch and breakfast, no matter their family income.

Let us extend this logic. If we set the poverty benchmark at 50 percent of a median household income (disposable), the analyst Shawn Fremstad calculates, the poverty line for one person would rise to $17,685 from $12,488 in 2017—an increase that Fremstad advocates to "keep pace with mainstream living standards over time." For a household of four, the poverty line would be $35,370 compared to the 2017 line of $25,094, about 40 percent higher.

Such levels are consistent with a 2016 survey done by Gallup in which the respondents said a "get-along" income is even higher than Fremstad suggests: for a family of four, $50,000 a year. Research into adequate living standards, including by the Economic Policy Institute, put a minimum adequate budget at a higher level than these. The consensus figure is around twice the official poverty measure. Even polling several years ago by the conservative think tank the American Enterprise Institute found that Americans think the poverty line is around $33,000 a year for a family of four.

Fremstad computes that at 50 percent of median income, the child poverty rate based on a new SPM-type calculation would have been more than 21 percent in 2017, or some 15 million children. At 60 percent of median income, commonly used in Europe as the unofficial poverty line, the child poverty rate would have been 31 percent. This would come to well more than 21 million children (compared as a reminder to the current official measure of 13 million). The actual poverty rate would have been still higher when including SPM deductions like medical expenses and work-related expenses like transportation and childcare.

As a reminder, 15.6 percent of children are reported as poor using the SPM, 17.5 percent under the official poverty line. Once we raise a poverty line above the SPM, the absolute number of poor children rises rapidly because family incomes begin to be taxed and government benefits per child start to be reduced. A rough calculation I made with a colleague suggests the poverty rate for black and Hispanic children would be around 50 percent if the poverty line were raised to 45 to 50 percent of median disposable income. These estimates are closer to reality than the rates calculated by our Census Bureau. In my view, they represent the true number of poor children of color in America.

In 2019, the Trump administration announced it planned to adopt an inflation measure that rises more slowly in calculating the poverty line. This would keep the rate lower, thus reporting fewer poor. There is some bipartisan support for such a change, said to be more accurate. But others note that it understates the rising price of products typically needed by the poor. The consequences of such a change are clear, however. Millions of people over time would lose access to food stamps, health assistance, and housing subsidies.

CHAPTER 8

MONEY MATTERS

Until recently, analysts, policymakers, and many of the rest of us thought the pronounced difficulties poor children face were the result of factors like single-parent families, bad prenatal health, poor nutrition, low levels of parental education, poor schools, crime-ridden neighborhoods, and frequent moving and evictions. This remains true. Recent research, however, has increasingly shown that low income itself is a key, and arguably the major, cause of the debilitating outcomes in cognition, emotional stability, and health for poor children. The countless studies reinforcing this claim are an important breakthrough.

The claim that poverty-level income explains many of the damaging hardships for children had long been challenged both by the political right and some mainstream analysts, but the impressive newer research has whittled away at these counterclaims. The new emphasis on the importance of money alone leads to proposed solutions that are more efficient at reducing poverty, the most effective of which, in my view and that of a growing number of academic experts, is an unconditional cash allowance for households with children.

As we've seen, poor children suffer hardships at a much higher rate than the non-poor. Now we know that there is growing evidence that universal cash transfers, money itself, can solve or mitigate many problems. After canvassing a wide variety of recent studies, a research team from the London School of Economics writes, "household income appears to affect a wide range of different outcomes at the same time. We have seen evidence of significant effects on parenting and the physical home environment, maternal depression, smoking during pregnancy, children's cognitive ability, achievement and engagement in school, and children's behaviour and anxiety."

PATHWAYS OF DAMAGE FROM LOW INCOME

Twenty years ago, it was not yet clear which channels led from poverty to damage. Jeanne Brooks-Gunn and Greg Duncan wondered in their influential 1997 report whether the damage done by poverty is "through inadequate nutrition; fewer learning experiences; instability of residence; lower quality of schools; exposure to environmental toxins, family violence, and homelessness; dangerous streets; or less access to friends, services, and, for adolescents, jobs?"

Newer research has focused on three pathways by which income poverty has led to damage. These pathways include, first, inadequate money for food, rent, heat, and other material necessities. With money one can buy nutritious food, larger and more stable housing, heat and electricity, toys, warm coats, eyeglasses, and regular visits to the doctor, including transportation.

But two other potent pathways are less obvious. Money also helps reduce family stress, which significantly affects children's prospects. Such stress results in parental depression, anger, neglect, drinking, taking drugs, and violence. Money also helps parents provide a psychologically nourishing, unchaotic environment in which learning and social development can germinate. They can buy books and computers, subscribe to an Internet provider, hire tutors, send children to special classes, pay for music or art lessons, and provide wholesome recreation. In our era, poor parents particularly cannot keep up with an America in which parents spend more and more on children's activities.

The absence of money measurably affects poor children's ability to reason and calculate, undermines emotional stability and self-control, and in general deleteriously affects health. Moreover, the longer children live below the poverty line, it is now clear, the worse the damage. The younger they are when they become poor, the greater the damage. Even children who are in poverty for a short time are adversely affected—and one in three children in America live in poverty for at least one year. One in twenty live in poverty for ten years or more.

Poverty also has long-term consequences as children turn into young adults. Fewer graduate high school or college, the wages they eventually earn are on average lower, and a highly disproportionate number of poor young men enter the prison system. At age fifty, people who spent some time in poverty as young children were significantly more likely to have high blood pressure, asthma, and diabetes than children who grew up in families with incomes more than twice the poverty line. They were 71 percent more likely to have a stroke or heart attack. Some disadvantages of poverty can likely be offset over time, but longer-term studies may reflect a circle of material disadvantage that continues to affect these children as they grow older.

The doubters continue to make their case that more cash welfare means more damage. As we've seen, the political right, in particular, focuses less on inadequate income than on genetics, parental character, dependency, and a culture of "bad habits," including out-of-wedlock childbirth, crime, laziness, disdain for school, and, in Oscar Lewis's famous accounts, the inability to delay gratification. According to these ideologues, government welfare programs—and it seems, in particular, more cash income—would contribute further to these destructive bad habits.

Even some who do not share what I consider the prejudices of the right question whether money or the lack of high-wage jobs are the main causal factors. A 1997 book by Susan Mayer was a well-researched example that challenged the assumptions about the direct line between poverty-level incomes and damage. Mayer writes, "Parental incomes are not as important to children's outcomes as many social scientists have thought. This is because the parental characteristics that employers value and are willing to pay for, such as skills, diligence, honesty, good health, and reliability, also improve children's life chances, independent of their effect on parents' income."

Analysts with aligned positions often support a wide range of solutions to child poverty like more housing subsidies, more professional home visitations, publicly financed childcare, early education, and crime prevention. Others emphasize behavioral, character-based issues as chief causes—not the lack of money— asserting that factors like young parentage and female-headed households are the primary causes of poverty and its hardships. In fact, many maintain poverty can be corrected without additional cash money for the poor.

The result has been a tendency to document a single hardship and propose a specific solution to fix it. The wide range of solutions proposed are usually valuable. But in my view, these many one-off solutions have turned out to be an encumbrance for reducing poverty sharply.

TRACING THE CAUSAL LINK TO MONEY

In the past two decades, scholars have done very well at parsing many interrelated factors to isolate the causal role of income itself. As Brooke-Gunn and Duncan wrote in 1997, these studies adjust for other factors, including, "statistically, the effects of maternal age at the child's birth, maternal education, marital status, ethnicity, and other factors on child outcomes."

These studies have isolated low income as the cause of damage to children in poverty by, for example, comparing cognitive and health outcomes for siblings who were raised at different times, when the family income had changed significantly. Those raised in periods when the family generally had more income performed better in measurable ways, such as on achievement tests, than their siblings did when family income was lower. The children who were raised when incomes were low also were less securely attached to parents and had higher levels of depression and shorter attention spans and were prone to behavioral problems such as frequent fighting.

Actually, we can find low income as the main cause of the hardships and damage of poverty by looking at the consequences of current welfare policies themselves. Government programs in which benefits have changed over time provide abundant data for isolating low incomes as a fundamental cause of problems.

NATURAL EXPERIMENTS

Variations in government programs, or the creation of new programs, create what scholars sometimes call natural experiments. This "exogenous" increase in incomes offers an opportunity to measure the consequences of sudden increases in benefits and income compared to periods when funding was lower, or compared to those families who did not get increases.

Two sets of government-expanded income programs offered among the most interesting examples of natural experiments about the impact of money. The benefits of the Earned Income Tax Credit, which are especially helpful for families with children, were generously raised in 1993. The value of the credit increased by 40 percent on average for families with one child and roughly 100 percent for those with two children.

Researchers estimated how much improvement there was for those children in families with significant increases in tax credit income, comparing them to those where incomes didn't rise as much. Such exogenous increases of income were separated from the effects of other potential coincident factors such as parental behavior or education. There were also increases in the EITC before 1993 and again in 2009 that add to the dataset on these issues. In addition, the state EITCs provided more information for analysis.

The results were a particularly fascinating affirmation that money makes a major difference. The children whose families had significant increases in EITC income as compared to those who did not had higher school grades and results on achievement tests, attended college in greater proportion, and were generally healthier. One study also showed that the birth weight of newborns was higher in these newly better-off families, and the stress level for mothers was also measurably reduced.

Looking back to the early 1970s, Richard Nixon proposed a guaranteed income program in the form of a "negative income tax" in order to continue but streamline the implementation of the War on Poverty. The lower the income of the poor family, the greater the tax refund benefits would be (to a maximum ceiling benefit); benefits would be distributed in the form of cash payments. It was a forerunner of the Earned Income Tax Credit. But in Nixon's case, even if a family earned no income, it would receive a cash stipend. Opponents were concerned that it would encourage individuals not to work.

Various localities experimentally implemented the negative income tax for brief periods. The results were encouraging. Little labor time was lost, it turned out, and in some cases there was no evidence of work shirking at all. But the Nixon proposal, passed by the House of Representatives, was defeated in the Senate. Nixon himself withdrew his support.

THE AMERICAN INDIAN CASINO

Years later, another set of studies on the positive effects of increased incomes for poor children attracted a great deal of attention. The American Indian tribes of North Carolina opened a casino in 1996 on the reservation of the Eastern Band of Cherokees. Each member of the Cherokee tribe was given a share of the casino's profits, paid every six months. Children's shares were placed into a bank account until they were eighteen. The contribution the first year averaged $4,000, but by 2006, when several studies of the consequences were complete, the annual contribution per person had reached $9,000.

Analyses showed that the payments improved educational achievement significantly for the average child compared to non-Indian families in neighboring communities (who received no additional support). The proportion graduating from high school increased substantially. The increase in income also reduced the chances of the children's committing a crime once they were teenagers. One study found that psychiatric disorders in adolescence and well into young adulthood were significantly lower than for those who had not received supplemental income.

CANADIAN CHILD ALLOWANCES

An early guaranteed income program in Canada opened a research avenue that showed clear benefits for families, including their children, and set the stage for future programs. A town in the Canadian province of Manitoba experimented with a guaranteed annual income from 1974 to 1978. Under the program, dubbed Mincome, the people of Dauphin, Manitoba, "were offered guaranteed incomes equivalent to $19,500 for a four-person household (the guarantee varied by household size). People earning no labor market income, for whatever reason, could access the full guarantee, which was about . . . 49 percent of median household income in 1976." Roughly 18 percent of Dauphinites—over 2,000 individuals, or roughly 700 households—received benefits at some point throughout the program. A study done many years after the program was terminated in 1978 proved eye-opening. A Canadian scholar found "that, overall, hospitalizations in Dauphin declined relative to the control group." Accidents and injuries also declined. The Canadian scholar Evelyn Forget of the University of Manitoba continued, "You can argue accident and injury hospitalizations are strongly related to poverty." Teenagers whose families received Mincome stayed in school longer.

Today's Canadian child allowances have also provided useful data for analyzing the impact of differing incomes on outcomes for poor children. Child cash payments differ by region. The results have been striking. Researchers found positive results for educational test scores and mental and physical health outcomes among those children whose families received higher allowances. Cognitive success was measured by achievement exams and school attainment levels. Mental and emotional health were measured in a number of ways, including observations about hyperactivity and social aggression. The researchers also assessed depression in mothers, thought to be a factor that can weigh on child performance. In all these cases, those families who received higher allowances showed substantial positive results compared to the others.

THE LONDON SCHOOL OF ECONOMICS REPORT

One of the most influential and thorough reports on the consequences of giving additional money to families with poor children, mentioned above, was undertaken by the researchers at the London School of Economics and published in 2013. The LSE researchers reviewed 44,000 studies of poverty's impact before they pared them down to thirty-four that they concluded truly isolated income as a determinant of outcomes. Among these dependable studies, income increases led to notably higher scores on achievement tests for children, more stable emotional behavior, and improved health. Only five of the chosen studies did not show a positive relationship between income and outcomes.

"Our review indicates clearly," the LSE researchers concluded, "that money makes a difference to children's outcomes. Poorer children have worse cognitive, social-behavioural and health outcomes in part *because they are poorer*, and not just because poverty is correlated with other household and parental factors. The evidence relating to cognitive development and school achievement is the clearest, followed by that on social and behavioural development."

A UNIQUE LONG-TERM STUDY

One historical study provided stunning evidence of *long-term* benefits of unconditional cash welfare. It involved the federal Mothers Pensions programs that were instituted in the early 1900s as part of the first wave of Progressive reforms in America. There had been widows' benefits more or less since the Civil War, but mothers' pensions were instituted at the turn of the century to help in raising children with decent nutrition and housing.

Researchers traced the outcomes for the children of the pension recipients until their eventual deaths, usually late in life. A summary published in 2016 found that these children lived one year longer than comparable children whose mothers did not receive the benefits. A year as an average for a large group is a long time, and many lived much longer. The researchers also found that the number of underweight infants in the pension groups was reduced sharply, the children attended school longer, and they were much less likely to drop out of high school, thereby earning higher wages.

HOME INVESTMENT AND HEALTH

More recently, a measure called the HOME scale has been developed to gauge how constructive the home environment is for children. It inventories the number of toys, books, and learning materials in the home. It also observes and measures parental practices at home. The lower the income, it has been found, the lower the ranking on this HOME scale.

According to one of the early surveys, low-income families spent about $880 (in 2012 dollars) per child annually, and higher-income families spent more than $3,700. By 2006–2007, while low-income families had increased their spending to $1,400, high-income families had increased theirs to $9,400. One study measured the impact of an extra $10,000 a year of income for poor children from birth to five years old, finding major positive impacts on cognitive achievement.

Several studies also show convincingly that low income itself—even when adjusted for family composition, the characteristics of parents, and other possible causal factors—increases the maltreatment of children.

For example, the Children's Bureau of the U.S. Administration for Children and Families (ACF) reports the number of instances of child protective services visits annually. Research concluded that one-quarter of child maltreatment was attributable to poverty, unemployment, and financial stress. Another study found that increases in the EITC led to reduced child maltreatment. Sexual and physical abuse of children, and exposure to domestic violence between adults, were most sensitive to economic factors.

A closer look at the thirty-four studies cited by the London School of Economics researchers provides still further evidence that more money given to needy parents leads to more investment in children. One study specifically found that as incomes rose, more books were read and more discussions took place with parents. Another study found that when income increased, parents spent more on children's clothing, toys, and fruits and vegetables, and less on alcohol and tobacco.

Three scholars—Hirokazu Yoshikawa, J. Lawrence Aber, and William Beardslee—similarly reviewed a range of contemporary research. They concluded: "On the basis of this selective review of key studies, we come to several major conclusions. First, the causal effect of family poverty, and to a lesser extent, neighborhood poverty, on worse child and youth M-E-B [mental, emotional and behavioral] health is well established. This causal effect provides a strong rationale for prevention based on poverty.... The [measured] effect of poverty is independent of associated factors such as levels of parental education or race/ethnicity; there is little evidence that the harmful impact of poverty on child or youth M-E-B health differs by race/ethnicity."

Based on analyses of how more income had closed the achievement gap with better-off children, the LSE group finds that half the achievement gap could be closed by an increase in family income of $10,000 a year. The growing evidence that money matters—that low income is the principal cause of material hardship—should be a guide to new, more efficient public policy and justify greater government spending.

CHAPTER 9

THE BEHAVIOR OF THE POOR IS NOT THE PRIORITY

The emphasis by so many poverty analysts on the irresponsible behavior of poor Americans has seriously undermined the nation's ability and willingness to deal with poverty fairly and thoroughly. With the virtual elimination of cash welfare in America, the deserving poor—that is, those who deserve government aid—are thought to be almost only those who work. Those who work but make very low wages are also out of favor under the new social philosophy, and many who now work make poverty wages. It bears repeating that, once the Clinton economic boom had passed, poverty rates *did not fall* after welfare reform.

To influential policy centrists or conservatives like Isabelle Sawhill and Ron Haskins, the source of poverty often pivots around poor unwed mothers. It seems completely obvious. Many of the poor are single mothers in America, and many single mothers are poor. So they should get married. The respected Sawhill even defended former vice president Dan Quayle when he famously criticized the TV character Murphy Brown in 1992 for having a child out of wedlock. She wrote about her own successful marriage in supporting Quayle, concluding "no government program is likely to reduce child poverty as much as bringing back marriage as the preferable way of raising children."

But as noted, a high level of out-of-wedlock births is a trend across rich nations. There is far less stigma attached to single motherhood or unwed female adults than in earlier decades. Even Sawhill concedes, "For women under age 30, more than half of babies are born out of wedlock. A lifestyle once associated with poverty has become mainstream." Women can now often pay their own way and actively seek careers, and are therefore less dependent on men. Young women who want a baby don't want a husband who is not right for them.

The economists George Akerlof and Janet Yellen have suggested another related possibility for unmarried births. As contraception and abortion became more accessible beginning in the 1970s (Massachusetts led the way then by legalizing the sale of contraception methods over the counter), the prevalence of "shotgun" marriages declined. If women got pregnant, they and their partners no longer felt obliged to get married.

The attack on welfare included in particular the highly charged claim that unmarried births were the result of a welfare program that rewarded mothers with more children. This accusation was usually leveled at black women. Some, therefore, argued that the reform of welfare in 1996 led to the reduction in unmarried births because women no longer received additional funding if they had more babies.

In fact, the proportion of unmarried mothers began to rise in the 1960s, well before the welfare wars. And after several years of TANF, there was no more traditional welfare, and the unmarried birth rates continued to rise in the 2000s. Regarding black women, the unmarried birth rate of black women more or less peaked by 1980. As Peter Edelman writes, "The growth in the rate of unmarried births in the United States over the past thirty years [since the 1980s] is almost entirely attributable to changes among whites and Hispanics."

The damage by unwanted births is not always a priority among those opposed to abortion. The rise in unwanted births among unmarried women seemed of little concern with state Republicans who passed extremely restrictive abortion regulations in 2018 and 2019. Restrictive abortion laws would add children to the nation's poverty count. In fact, in recent years the loosening of abortion restraints led to fewer children of unmarried mothers.

Other behavioral attributes of the poor also shaped the policy response of many child poverty experts. Those parents who didn't finish high school were singled out, as discussed further below.

THE BEHAVIOR OF THE AMERICAN POOR
IS NOT UNIQUE

There is an assumption even among trained academics that the types of behavior that they think cause poverty in America are unique to this country. One reason this attitude is not seen as bias has to do with the lack of studies of similar behavior in other rich nations with lower poverty rates. Three sociologists, David Brady,

Ryan Finnigan, and Sabine Hübgen, completed such a comparison in 2017. Doing a thorough literature search, they found that there are specifically four major individual characteristics that a consensus of economists and other analysts consider major causes of poverty in America. I have alluded to a couple previously. The four are single motherhood, low education attainment, high unemployment, and young heads of families.

Brady and his colleagues explored how prevalent the behavioral characteristics are in other rich nations. In what must come as a surprise to many poverty analysts, they find that the *average* proportion (what they term prevalences) of the poorly educated, the unemployed, young household headship, and single mothers in the United States is often *below* that of the other nations, according to data on twenty-nine rich democracies, compiled by the Luxembourg Income Study. And yet American poverty is significantly higher than in all the major rich nations with arguably "bad" behavior.

As Brady and his colleagues summarize: "Scholars routinely ask why the poor fail to get married, why they do not complete their educations, and why they do not work. Given [that] the U.S. actually has below average 'prevalences' of [such] risks, our results show U.S. residents tend to make fewer such choices and engage in fewer such behaviors than those in other rich democracies."

As for single-female-headed families, which attract the most attention, the American proportion of about 8 percent of all families is only slightly higher than the average overseas. The U.S. proportion is lower than in the United Kingdom and Ireland, where childhood poverty is less common. The proportion of children in the United States living with a head of household still in their teenage years or early twenties was about 6 percent—lower than in Denmark, Norway, and Sweden, where childhood poverty is rare. "The proportion of [American] children living with a single mother and no other potential earners is not unusual in comparative terms," conclude the social scientists Patrick Heuveline and Matthew Weinshenker, in another study. "This immediately renders highly dubious the hypothesis that reducing single parentage will reduce poverty significantly for children or anyone else."

Such is the case for the behavioral fixes for poverty regularly advanced by consensus economists and policy analysts. What makes the difference in childhood poverty in rich democracies other than the United States is that owing to generous and well-targeted social policies such as free or inexpensive childcare, paid family leave, low-cost preschool, easy access to healthcare, and monthly cash benefits, single mothers are not as poor on average as they are in America.

These highly criticized behavioral characteristics don't generate as much adult poverty in other nations due to the availability of jobs, higher wages, job training and apprenticeships, and generous social policies, including far more extensive unemployment insurance.

A good example is lower educational attainment. For those with lower levels of education in particular, Americans face a far higher likelihood of poverty than in other nations. "If you lack a high school degree in the United States," wrote Brady, Finnigan, and Hübgen recently, "it increases the probability of your being in poverty by 16.4 percent. In the 28 other rich democracies, a lack of education increases the probability of poverty by less than 5 percent on average." One reason, of course, is the rapid decline of high-wage and union jobs in manufacturing and many other sectors in the United States—and the lack of policies to compensate for this decline.

Race and ethnicity in America do not change these conclusions. The general disadvantages of people of color in the job market, lack of jobs and childcare, and inadequate coverage of other social policies are more significant causes of poverty than a higher incidence of single motherhood.

Most telling, scholars have shown statistically that reducing allegedly "poverty-causing" behavioral risks does not reduce poverty rates. Reducing the proportion of single mothers in America to the levels of 1970 and the 1980s, according to Brady and colleagues, would have a negligible effect on reducing poverty levels.

Much of the moralistic attitude Brady and colleagues debunk harkens back to Daniel Patrick Moynihan and the black-female-headed family. In a 2001 PBS interview, a few years after the welfare reform debates, Moynihan illustrated his bias starkly. He said, "My view is we had stumbled onto a major social change in the circumstances of postmodern society. It was not long ago in this past century that an anthropologist working in London—a very famous man at the time, [Bronisław]

Malinowski—postulated what he called the first rule of anthropology: that in all known societies, all male children have an acknowledged male parent. That's what we found out everywhere." But this assumption, just like the "culture of poverty" argument Moynihan had helped raise to the level of common sense for a generation of policymakers, has not stood the test of time.

Edin and her colleagues in sociology, as we've suggested, have demonstrated that poor black and Latina women who have children without marrying a man were not alone: in fact, they were part of a growing norm, a general cultural shift against marriage as an institution. Parenting without marriage is so appealing ideologically as the moralistic explanation of poverty that simple facts are ignored. In fact, many married couples are poor. As Shawn Fremstad writes, "Among parents living below the poverty line and caring for minor children, 43 percent are married. . . . There are more married parents with incomes below the poverty line than there are never-married ones, and more food-insecure adults live in households with children headed by married couples than in ones headed by just a man or woman."

As Kristi Williams, an Ohio State sociologist, concludes, "The problem is that there's no evidence that the kind of marriages that poor, single parents enter into will have these same benefits [as those of the middle class]."

Behavioral fixes, it's clear, are not the answer advocates claim. What can we do, then, to reduce childhood poverty in the United States—and what can we do to end it?

CHAPTER 10

WHAT TO DO

To repeat: I believe we should provide monthly, substantial, and unconditional cash allowances for all children through disbursements to their families. It is long past time to recognize that well-meaning policy advocates have not been able to cut child poverty to the levels promised, in particular for the very poor. That is not to say, there has not been substantial success in cutting poverty. Some claim, even progressives, the child poverty rate has fallen by half since the 1960s. A more likely reduction is 20 to 25 percent. But even if the more dramatic poverty reduction were correct, the child poverty rate in America remains tragically high and the damage to the economy towering.

We have seen research studies and natural experiments that show increased monthly income improves the health and the cognitive and emotional abilities of children, with likely effects well into adulthood. We have noted the considerable success of many other nations that have long provided child cash allowances, and examine this further below. We know that because of the reduction or elimination of longstanding cash welfare programs, the very poor are badly neglected. It is time to right the unbalanced scales of decency.

The coming together of several strands of research about child poverty make a powerful case for cash allowances. Two stand out. Independent analyses, as we shall see, demonstrate that a reasonable cash allowance per child of $300 or $400 a month can reduce child poverty by half. The second is the success of unconditional cash programs without strings attached in Europe and Canada, which shows us that the large majority of parents care about their children and typically do not squander the money on themselves.

FOCUS, COMMITMENT, SIMPLICITY— AND IMMEDIACY

I have discussed the various theories about the overstatement of behavioral causes of poverty not merely because they are usually wrong but also because they distract from more practical solutions. Part of my purpose is to set aside moralistic thinking about marriage, teenage sex, shirking of work, and racial characteristics. Reliable research, as I've pointed out, suggests that these are not the potent causes of poverty many are prone to believe.

Substantial cash allowances provided monthly to all families with children do not exclude other efforts. The creation of jobs and support for wages for low-income workers, through infrastructure investment, apprenticeships, and wage and work subsidies, makes eminent good sense. Mothers can greatly benefit from more childcare support. More and better education, including vocational education, can be critical. Housing subsidies have proven especially valuable, with measurable benefits for poor children. Some studies show stable and decent housing can be an especially important variable for children's well-being. Democrats in recent years have offered a variety of aggressive programs that touch on many of these issues, notably housing. But often well-intentioned advocates propose an all-court press of policies, which is politically unwieldy. Cash allowances can cover many of these problems and should be given priority because they can cut child poverty quickly and efficiently. A main reason other wealthy nations have sharply lowered child poverty rates is that almost all of them provide cash allowances, without conditions, to *all* children. Austria, Belgium, Bulgaria, Canada, Denmark, Estonia, Finland, France, Germany, Hungary, Ireland, Latvia, Luxembourg, the Netherlands, Poland, Romania, Slovakia, Sweden, and the UK all do so. The allowances are typically available whether parents work or not.

As of 2016, Canada had a base child allowance of $4,935 per child under six and $4,164 per child aged six to seventeen, but there is a variation among regions in Canada. The benefit for two children in Brussels is about $3,700 a year, and in Germany $5,200; in Ireland $3,750, and in the Netherlands about $2,815.

Can cash allowances succeed in America? The anger toward cash welfare in the 1980s and 1990s was underlined by a nationwide attitude that the poor, and perhaps especially blacks, would squander cash they receive, abuse the system to get more welfare, or shirk work.

Will parents spend a child allowance on improving prospects for their children or on themselves? Consider the aggressive childcare program begun in Britain in 1998 that included a cash allowance for children. Scholars have scrutinized the effects of the program, including the cash allowances, on poor parents' investments in their children. Child poverty rates fell sharply. The economists Paul Gregg, Jane Waldfogel, and Elizabeth Washbrook reported significant increases in spending on children's needs.

A study of similar welfare reform on family spending in the United States found the money mostly went to work-related expenses, as these programs required mothers to work. The Conservative government in Britain, wielding the sword of austerity, reversed some of these benefits in recent years, and child poverty in Britain rose.

There is other persuasive evidence that parents will spend extra money on children's needs. The natural experiments cited earlier, such as mothers' government pensions, increases in EITC, and the Indian casino examples, show that extra money went to the support of children, whose outcomes were measurably improved over groups that didn't receive the money.

There is also a coming together of conservative and progressive thought on this issue, though with some dangerous implications. Conservatives, such as the libertarian Niskanen Institute, prefer reducing government's patronizing control of the poor by providing cash that the poor can decide how to use. But these libertarians simultaneously call for a reduction in needed social programs. Charles Murray advocates eliminating all welfare programs and providing an annual cash grant of $10,000 a year to Americans over twenty-one.

The best proposals, in my view, must expand Americans' social rights—the childhood grant can supplement existing programs. It may also set a model for a new set of universal initiatives. There is bold precedent for universal policies for children in our past: the United States notably adopted free, public, and compulsory primary education in the nineteenth century.

Some antipoverty programs surely stigmatize the poor. By contrast, providing cash enables the poor to manage themselves without patronization. This is a major reason I'd advocate an unconditional child allowance, in contrast to many of those in Latin America, which require that parents meet educational and health requirements in order to receive money. Mexico is a prominent example.

As we've seen, an ongoing complaint of the right is that the remaining programs—Medicaid, SNAP, and housing subsidies—encourage Americans to shirk work just as the old cash welfare system did. It is the same story they told in the 1980s and 1990s, but the right relentlessly carries on despite the dramatic reduction in cash welfare. Most would no doubt have even more vociferous objections to a child cash allowance program.

Paul Ryan irresponsibly said as late as 2018, before

he retired as Speaker of the House, "Washington has spent trillions of dollars on dozens of programs to fight poverty. But we have barely moved the needle." As we know, child poverty has fallen if not adequately. The Trump Council on Economic Advisers made still more irresponsible claims a couple of months later, though with the help of statistical manipulation, that poverty has been almost eliminated!

Evidence shows strongly that social programs have at most a minor influence on Americans' willingness to work. The Trump White House economists produced a poverty report in the summer of 2018 to make their case for work requirements on Medicaid, SNAP, and housing subsidies. Its analysis is shoddy and misleading. They claim that many able people who receive Medicaid do not work, for instance. But the Kaiser Family Foundation found that 60 percent of the recipients had full- or part-time jobs, and an additional 18 percent lived in a family with a working adult. We know that three out of four SNAP recipients in any month work within a year before or after taking benefits, often that very month. Half of SNAP recipients were working when they received the benefits.

A study by economists of cash allowances in more than half a dozen developing nations—the Philippines, Indonesia, Morocco, Mexico, Nicaragua, and Honduras—could find no fall in employment numbers when these allowances were introduced.

TANF has provided a grim real-world example of what happens when cash payments are significantly cut. While many women got jobs, as required, most of those jobs were unstable or faded away in time. And many women could not get jobs due to education inadequacies, lack of transportation, and little help with childcare. The study by Arloc Sherman and Danilo Trisi concluded that "between 1995 (before the welfare law was enacted) and 2005 (a year with similar unemployment), the share of children in deep poverty rose from 2.1 percent to 3.0 percent, and the number of such children jumped from 1.5 million to 2.2 million [based on adjusted data, different than the OPM and somewhat different than the SPM]. Similarly, the deep poverty rate among people in female-headed families jumped from 2.9 percent in 1995 to 6.0 percent in 2005."

Scholars writing in the 1980s, including the child poverty analyst Greg Duncan and the political scientist Mary Corcoran, had seemingly put to rest claims that welfare led to destructive dependencies on a wide scale. These studies were based on detailed analysis of government surveys and employment trends.

A point I raised earlier bears repeating. In the 1980s and 1990s, a "new consensus" came together with the critical participation of economists from Harvard and other centrist or formerly progressive economists who developed research in support of the claim, contrary to Duncan and Corcoran, that welfare led to dependencies. In their analysis, among other causes of poverty, single motherhood ranked high, with all its racist (and classist) overtones, and cash payments could be destructive and ultimately costly. David Ellwood of Harvard was a prominent leader in advocating a work requirement for welfare, targeting women. Ellwood and Mary Jo Bane, also of Harvard, analyzed the longer-term data but used a different methodology than Duncan and others to arrive at how many long-term poor were on welfare. On any given day, the study found that a high proportion of participants were long term and costly, arguably justifying the claim of dependency. On this basis, they advocated a work requirements program. But the analysis did not mean a high proportion of those ever receiving welfare were long-term. In fact, they were not. To the contrary, the simulations showed there were many more short-term participants. These progressive advocates supported the new Clinton welfare reform, but at least they also thought a jobs creation program was necessary.

TANF was passed without such a jobs program when President Clinton, who originally supported a jobs program, yielded to Republican pressure. The House had just won an overwhelming Republican majority. With the work of William Julius Wilson, Herbert Gans, and others, the cultural accusation of irresponsibility launched at unmarried women, and black women in particular, was carefully and convincingly rebutted. But TANF had become law, and cash welfare was almost entirely ended in America. Work requirements did not reduce general poverty; the expanded EITC and SNAP, and the new CTC, did so. In later research, it was shown that jobs taken due to TANF often paid low wages. In the meantime, more Americans became very poor, often even when they worked. Without AFDC, as noted, many received almost no help at all aside from SNAP. Social supports for the aged and disabled grew rapidly, while growing far more slowly for single mothers with children. As a reminder, an expanded Social Security Disability program was passed in 1965 and kept growing, becoming a major source of controversy in recent years.

MAINSTREAM SUPPORT

More mainstream researchers are moving in the direction of support for unconditional cash allowances for not merely the poor but for all children. These allowances would be taxable, and thus higher-income families would receive less on balance per child. Meanwhile, the child allowance proposal directly reaches the very poor.

To generate a new national conviction, one of the first steps would be to acknowledge the size of the problem and the significant funds needed to come to terms with it. As an example, the British undertook their aggressive program under the Labour prime ministers Tony Blair and Gordon Brown. One part of it was the development of Head Start–type programs across the nation, a project called Sure Start, at a cost of $12 billion in additional government spending. Such a program in America, scaled up to size with dozens of new centers, would cost America an estimated $160 billion.

In the UK, the child poverty rate before figuring in government programs and taxes was higher than America's, some 34 percent according to the Luxembourg Income Study. But government policies, including the child cash allowance noted above, reduced the poverty rate by 25 percentage points in England, before recent austerity measures imposed by the Conservative government. The result is that relative child poverty in the UK was only 9 percent, compared to 21 percent (measured the way Britain does) in the United States.

America has not developed an adequate new program of such scope. To the contrary, until recently, there has been inadequate attention paid to child poverty, as demonstrated by the small share of social spending going to families below the poverty line. This attitude has begun to change slightly; the Child Tax Credit, for example, was increased to $2,000. As the scholar Neal Halfon said while comparing recent American child welfare policy with its British equivalents, "Irrespective of their professed commitment to young children, the Obama administration was only able to allocate a small percentage of that amount to a range of early childhood programs—in bits and pieces—in different legislative bills, which were not aligned or integrated into a coherent cross-agency strategy." The general attitude has begun to change slightly, as the increase in the Child Tax Credit to $2,000 shows. New, more aggressive policy proposals for children are being introduced by Democrats, which generally increase the amount refundable among other changes. It does not mean they will become law.

REDUCING POVERTY BY HALF

By focusing on cash allowances alone, it is feasible to pay each family with children enough to truly reduce child poverty by half, and to do so quickly. A universal payment would also raise the incomes of those now defined as near-poor by the government, but who I would argue are truly poor. We also know that families with incomes near the middle of the pack are struggling as well in an era of stagnating incomes. Such an allowance would help them. Families with children under six could be paid more, as research shows that they can benefit most from more investment.

I believe that tax credits, seemingly Democrats' favorite tool, should be given a lower priority, since they are usually distributed only annually (at tax time), they often require a lot of paperwork, and the benefits are skewed away from the poorest. Moreover, conditional child allowances, as implemented in several South American nations during the "Pink Tide" wave of left-populist governments from the late 1990s to about 2015–18, required parents to meet education and health-care standards for children. Such demands can be cumbersome and patronizing, assuming parents cannot decide what their own children need. Conditional allowances are often humiliating, when antipoverty programs should be reducing shame.

At my own small think tank, the Bernard L. Schwartz Rediscovering Government Initiative housed at the long-standing Century Foundation, we contracted a well-recognized Columbia University team of social scientists and economists to analyze the benefits of reducing poverty using several different levels of cash aid for poor children in lieu of a tax credit.

The Columbia researchers tested ten alternative policies involving different levels of cash allowances for either all children under six, or all children under eighteen. Their costs ranged from under $100 billion to $200 billion a year. In the testing, the cash allowances were universal, going to all children no matter how poor or rich. These alternative options also assumed that the Child Tax Credit was eliminated.

Against this universalist approach, they also tested more generous levels of the CTC that were completely redeemable. In other words, parents of poor children received money even if they didn't earn adequately to produce a sufficient liability. As noted, the current CTC does not usually reach the very poor, as it is a credit against earnings—the very poor don't qualify for any substantial credit because their wages are too low. Meantime, those couples earning up to $400,000 a year now qualify for a portion of the CTC due to Trump reforms.

The advantage of a universal childhood grant over an expanded Child Tax Credit was crystal-clear in the Columbia report. For every dollar the government spent, the Columbia analysis found, the poverty rate would fall more with the cash allowances than under an expanded CTC. For example, the scholars found that if a $2,500 annual cash disbursement was provided for every child in America under eighteen while the CTC was eliminated, the child poverty rate would drop to 11.4 percent, lifting 5.5 million children out of poverty, and deep poverty would be cut by 2.3 percent compared to the current CTC's effect of 0.2 percent. The total cost would be $109 billion.

In the most generous program tested, a $4,000

annual payment to all children under eighteen, overall child poverty would be cut by nearly 60 percent and deep poverty by some two-thirds. The cost would be roughly $200 billion a year.

Those who say this is politically unpalatable should be reminded we spend nearly $1 trillion a year on Social Security to cut the elderly poverty rate sharply—it is a model for universal social rights, as would be a childhood allowance for all.

MAINSTREAM ECONOMISTS AND A UNIVERSAL CHILDHOOD ALLOWANCE

A respected group of child poverty economists has since proposed a thoroughgoing universal child allowance. These are largely mainstream economists and analysts, including the aforementioned Columbia scholars Jane Waldfogel and David Harris and other leading child poverty experts, among them Greg Duncan and Luke Shaefer. They proposed a universal cash allowance of $3,000 a year to replace the CTC, and $3,600 for children under six.

The aim, as noted, is to reach more children in deep poverty and also create a floor of stability, especially in an era of unstable incomes, for less poor and even middle-income families. The program is meant to go to all families, regardless of income. The income would be subject to federal and local income taxes.

The scholars believe that $250 to $300 per child would cover the monthly cash shortfall of the average poor child. Their calculation is fairly moderate, but it would nevertheless be of considerable help. The subsidy is reduced with every additional child because there are economies of scale in a family—it takes less per child to raise two than one, or three than two. Higher allowances for younger children reflect their greater needs and their rapid learning at these ages, and parents of young children are typically poorer than those with older children.

The scholars found that giving $3,000 apiece to all children and eliminating the $4,000 income tax exemption per child would reduce the poverty rate for children by 43 percent, and deep poverty would fall by half. Net of eliminating the income tax exemption and the CTC, the scholars' proposal of $3,000 a year would cost taxpayers $93 billion.

Families would receive their money through a monthly electronic system. Once the nation acknowledges the need for cash allowances for kids, it can debate the size and distribution of the benefits. But cash allowances are, for now, the silver bullet we need.

Cutting child poverty in half would be a great victory for an American nation whose attitudes toward poverty have been generally skeptical. It would profoundly reduce the cognitive, neurological, and emotional disadvantages of poor children, substantially improve child health on average, raise the downtrodden esteem of these children, and have constructive long-term consequences. It would benefit virtually all Americans by restoring a large portion of the $1 trillion lost to GDP each year.

A still newer set of programs, including child cash allowances but also a wide range of other programs, was proposed by these and other scholars in a report in 2019 for the National Academies of Sciences, Engineering and Medicine. The report is a response to a mandate to suggest programs that would reduce poverty, and its goal is to reduce child poverty more gradually than the academic studies above. But all the proposals include a cash allowance.

EPILOGUE: FAITH IN THE POOR

There is much else to be done beyond child allowances, but as I've stressed the danger is to let a not-yet-politically practicable comprehensive agenda become an obstacle to a practical and beneficial one. Nevertheless, we must imagine a better world if we are to make one.

SNAP should be expanded, and include more generous programs for individuals without children as well.

High on any list of additional needs is a jobs creation program. Basing policies on a nostalgic view of past job growth, and an unawareness of true economic conditions today, is apt to go wrong.

We must also recognize that we now live in an era of almost universal female employment, partly created by poverty policies that demand work. But women and men do not have adequate paid leave for raising their children, or programs to care for them.

Truly universal public childcare remains elusive even where these programs have advanced furthest, as Ajay Chaudry has documented in New York City. More work must be done on equalizing pay with men and reducing evident prejudice against all women.

A major market failure in America is the lack of

construction of low-income housing for poor Americans. The private market won't solve this problem, so government must. The two federally assisted housing programs, public housing construction and Section 8 subsidies to rent in the private market, have proven valuable. But they reach too few people. Expanding such programs would help poor children perhaps the most. As noted, inadequate housing has a profound effect on children's lives.

Congressional attention is at last being directed at helping poor children. A bill was proposed by Senators Michael Bennett and Sherrod Brown in 2017 to establish a $3,000 allowance for all children six to eighteen and $3,600 for children under six, based on the Child Tax Credit. It would be refundable. This is close to a pure cash allowance: all children, even if their parents make no income, would be allocated $3,000, paid in monthly installments of $250 a month for older children and $300 a month for toddlers and pre-K-age kids. Its annual cost after eliminating the current CTC would be around $100 billion. Congresswoman Rosa De Lauro has proposed a similar bill.

Many Democrats have made proposals that involve forms of cash allowances. Let's begin to reduce the pain and disadvantage of poor children with an income program that will have immediate and extremely beneficial effects. Some will always complain that such cash welfare will create dependency. But we know such consequences are exaggerated and the immense gains for poor children are well worth this relatively negligible social cost.

There is no need to wait for the passage of other,

more politically difficult to realize programs to help the young. The nation is held back by the deep prejudice against cash welfare that continues to be reinforced by some scholars and right-wing think tanks. As the University of Michigan policy scholar Luke Shaefer says, "If you were going to choose one program, nothing is more effective than child allowances."

THE POTENTIAL OF THE POOR

We must develop an appreciation of the potential of poor Americans. That the United States refuses to raise those in poverty to a decent life reflects a mean-spirited and destructive prejudice against the poor, underlined by racism and a sense of class superiority. It's time to reeducate ourselves. As one of Amartya Sen's acolytes has put it, Sen believes "poverty is unfreedom."

The purpose of accurate poverty measures is to help the nation make decisions about where to invest in its citizenry, how to reduce pain and suffering, how to produce access to the opportunity so often promised by America, and what its moral obligation is—an obligation to equal opportunity, freedom of choice, and healthy lives. It is also necessary to understand what is needed to maintain a productive workforce and a prosperous economy—time to recognize the toll child poverty takes on the finances of all Americans in lost income due to reduced productivity across the economy and higher costs of social programs. This penalty can be sharply reduced, as, more important, can the pain of the lives that poor children inevitably face.

Mollie Orshansky said in the 1960s that her poverty line was not the line above which people will escape from hardship—rather, it is a line below which one should not have to live. America has dedicated itself to measuring poverty as a matter of mere subsistence. It is a cruel collective decision.

Tens of millions of Americans live below the minimal poverty line today. Measured by a fairer and updated line, the true number of deprived is around 60 million. The number of truly poor children is arguably more than 20 million. It is a cruel irony that we can't agree on how many poor Americans there are, no less cut the number. Let's change the national attitude—and recognize the reality of childhood poverty in this country. Cutting child poverty in half with a universal child allowance would be one of America's great moral victories.

ACKNOWLEDGMENTS

First, I must thank the hundreds of dedicated scholars and policy analysts who have spent a good part of their lives studying child poverty in America. When I started researching this book, I had no idea of the numbers of researchers and the quality of work they did. There are few nobler causes. There should be an annual financial prize for the best research done on child poverty that more fully recognizes these contributions.

Second, I thank Alfred A. Knopf for supporting my work over the years, and this book in particular, whose subject is dense and not readily accessible. They believe in the work. I owe particular thanks to Jon Segal, my editor, who had a major hand in crafting this book into a cohesive and readable whole, as he did previous books of mine. I also again must express appreciation to the head of Knopf, Sonny Mehta, for his constant support. I also thank Tracy White and Lakshman Achuthan for their intense interest in child poverty and the generous grant to me made by their foundation, the Rodney L. White Foundation.

Third, I must thank my superb researcher, the historian and scholar Joel Feingold, for his invaluable work in checking the facts, proposing additions, and diligently gathering sources for the project. An author he works with calls him "crackerjack." He is right.

For years now, I have been wholeheartedly thanking Charlotte Sheedy, my insightful literary agent, who has supported all of my projects with matchless enthusiasm, provided needed advice, and secured the best publishers for my work.

As I say, there are countless important researchers in this field, and I won't cite any here because I will leave too many out. They are mentioned in the text and in the endnotes. But several professional friends have provided support and valuable advice, including James Silberman, Louis Uchitelle, and Sanjay Reddy. I should add my daughter, Matina Madrick, a social policy analyst, for her frequent advice on various subjects.

I must also thank Bernard L. Schwartz for supporting my work at the Schwartz Rediscovering Government Initiative at the Century Foundation for many years now. The Century Foundation also valuably supported the early work we did on child poverty. The Century researcher Clio Chang made excellent contributions, and many on the Century staff provided needed support.

Finally, my incomparably energetic and wise wife, Kim Baker, was my foundation through what was a longer period of research and assimilation than I anticipated. As always, she read draft after draft and provided insight after insight.

NOTES

CHAPTER 1: INVISIBLE AMERICANS

3 In 1962, Michael Harrington published *The Other America:* Michael Harrington, *The Other America* (New York: Macmillan, 1962).

3 Under President Lyndon Johnson, the country adopted: Annelise Orleck and Lisa Gayle Hazirjian, eds., *The War on Poverty: A New Grassroots History, 1964–1980* (Athens: University of Georgia Press, 2011).

4 There are roughly 13 million officially poor children in America: Jessica L. Semega, Kayla R. Fontenot, and Melissa A. Kollar, *Income and Poverty in the United States: 2017* (Washington, DC: United States Census Bureau, 2018), 14.

4 In France and Germany only around one in ten children: Timothy Smeeding and Céline Thévenot, "Addressing Child Poverty: How Does the United States Compare with Other Nations?" *Academic Pediatrics* 16 (3S) (April 2016), S67–S75, S68.

4 according to the latest studies: H. Luke Shaefer, "The Kids Are Infrequently Alright: Material Hardship among Children in the United States." Unpublished manuscript, 2019.

5 Overwhelming evidence makes clear: Gary W. Evans and Pilyoung Kim, "Childhood Poverty and Health: Cumulative Risk Exposure and Stress Dysregulation," *Psychological Science* 18 (11) (November 2007), 953–57; Gary W. Evans

and Rochelle C. Cassells, "Childhood Poverty, Cumulative Risk Exposure, and Mental Health in Emerging Adults," *Clinical Psychological Science* 2 (3) (May 2014), 287–96; Adam Schickedanz, Benard P. Dreyer, and Neal Halfon, "Childhood Poverty: Understanding and Preventing the Adverse Impacts of a Most-Prevalent Risk to Pediatric Health and Well-Being," *Pediatric Clinics of North America* 62 (5) (October 2015), 1111–35; and Daniel T. Lichter, "Poverty and Inequality among Children," *Annual Review of Sociology* 23 (1997), 121–45.

5 They often live in physical and emotional pain: Bridget J. Goosby, "Early Life Course Pathways of Adult Depression and Chronic Pain," *Journal of Health and Social Behavior* 54 (1) (March 2013), 75–91.

5 Infant mortality is higher in the United States: U.S. Department of Health and Human Services, Marian F. MacDorman, T. J. Mathews, Ashna D. Mohangoo, and Jennifer Zeitlin, "International Comparisons of Infant Mortality and Related Factors: United States and Europe, 2010," *National Vital Statistics Reports* 63 (5) (September 2014), 1.

6 A stunning recent analysis finds that GDP is up to $1 trillion: Michael McLaughlin and Mark R. Rank, "Estimating the Economic Cost of Childhood Poverty in the United States," *Social Work Research* 42 (2) (June 2018), 73–83.

6 A universal program will also cover those children: Amartya Sen, "The Political Economy of Targeting," paper presented at Annual Bank Conference on Development Economics, World Bank (Washington, DC: 1992), in Dominique van de Walle and Kimberly Nead, eds., *Public Spending and the Poor: Theory and Evidence* (Washington, DC: World Bank, 1995), 11–24.

7 Several strands of research over the past twenty years: H. Luke Shaefer, Sophie Collyer, Greg Duncan, Kathryn Edin, Irwin Garfinkel, David Harris, Timothy M.

Smeeding, et al., "A Universal Child Allowance: A Plan to Reduce Poverty and Income Instability among Children in the United States," *RSF: The Russell Sage Foundation Journal of the Social Sciences* 4 (2) (February 2018), 22–42, and Joe VerValin, "The Case for a Universal Child Allowance in the United States," *Cornell Policy Review* (October 5, 2018), 1–4. See also Matt Bruenig, "Child Allowance," in People's Policy Project, *Family Fun Pack* (Washington, DC: People's Policy Project, 2019). Bruenig argues that a monthly child allowance of $300 should be part and parcel of a new set of social rights including parental leave, a universal gift of a "baby box" to new parents, free childcare, free pre-K, free healthcare, and free school lunch. My view is that such an all-court press dissipates political support. Efforts for a cash allowance would be more productive.

7 The research has partly been based on experiments: Lauren E. Jones, Kevin S. Milligan, and Mark Stabile, "Child Cash Benefits and Family Expenditures: Evidence from the National Child Benefit," *National Bureau of Economic Research Working Paper* 21101 (2015), 1–41; Samuel Hammond and Robert Orr, "Toward a Universal Child Benefit," *Niskanen Center: Reports* (October 2016), 1–13; and Barbara Wolfe, Jessica Jakubowski, Robert Haveman, and Marissa Courey, "The Income and Health Effects of Tribal Casino Gaming on American Indians," *Demography* 49 (2) (May 2012), 499–524.

7 Provocative historical sociology studies on cash relief programs: Anna Aizer, Shari Eli, Joseph Ferrie, and Adriana Lleras-Muney, "The Long Term Impact of Cash Transfers to Poor Families," *National Bureau of Economic Research Working Paper* 20103 (2014), 1–42.

8 Enabling families to use cash as they choose: Kevin Milligan and Mark Stabile, "Child Benefits, Maternal Employment, and Children's Health: Evidence from Canadian Child Benefit Expansions," *American Economic Review* 99

(2) (May 2009), 128–32, and Horacio Levy, Manos Matsaganis, and Holly Sutherland, "Towards a European Union Child Basic Income? Within and between Country Effects," *International Journal of Microsimulation* 6 (1) (2013), 63–85.

8 Some scholars believe poverty can be cut in half: Greg Duncan and Suzanne Le Menestrel, eds., *A Roadmap to Reducing Child Poverty* (Washington, DC: National Academies of Sciences, Engineering, and Medicine, 2019), 6–15.

9 Even food stamps have a work requirement: Robert Pear, "Thousands Could Lose Food Stamps as States Restore Pre-Recession Requirements," *New York Times*, April 1, 2016, and U.S. Department of Agriculture Food and Nutrition Service, "Able-Bodied Adults Without Dependents (ABAWDs): SNAP Supports Work," fns.usda.gov (July 17, 2018).

9 Studies have found that tax credits: Bruce D. Meyer, "The Effects of the Earned Income Tax Credit and Recent Reforms," in Jeffrey R. Brown, ed., *Tax Policy and the Economy*, vol. 24 (Chicago: University of Chicago Press, 2010), 153–80, 168.

9 It's growing in formerly rich suburbs: Long Island Association, *Poverty on Long Island: It's Growing* (Melville, NY: Long Island Association, 2017).

10 It's now near the national average: Catholic Charities of Santa Clara County and Step Up Silicon Valley, "Poverty in the Valley," stepupsv.org (2014).

10 It remains in the Deep South and the agricultural Southwest: Joseph Dalaker, *Poverty in the United States in 2017: In Brief* (Washington, DC: Congressional Research Service, 2018).

10 "There are now more census tracts of concentrated poverty": Paul Jargowsky, "Concentration of Poverty in the New Millennium: Changes in the Prevalence, Composition, and Location of High-Poverty Neighborhoods," *Century Foundation: Social Insurance* (December 18, 2013).

10 the child poverty rate is 17.5 percent: Semega, Fontenot, and Kollar, *Income and Poverty in the United States: 2017*, 12.

10 An updated alternative poverty measure: Liana Fox, *The Supplemental Poverty Measure: 2017* (Washington, DC: United States Census Bureau, 2018).

10 More than one out of three American children: Caroline Ratcliffe, *Child Poverty and Adult Success* (Washington, DC: Urban Institute, 2015).

11 The proportion of single-mother households in Europe: David Brady, Ryan M. Finnigan, and Sabine Hübgen, "Rethinking the Risks of Poverty: A Framework for Analyzing Prevalences and Penalties," *American Journal of Sociology* 123 (3) (November 2017), 740–86.

11 But American social programs raise twice as many elderly: Hilary W. Hoynes and Diane Whitmore Schanzenbach, "Safety Net Investments in Children," *National Bureau of Economic Research Working Paper* 24594 (2018), 1–44.

11 The Agriculture Department's measure of food insecurity: Alisha Coleman-Jensen, Matthew P. Rabbitt, Christian A. Gregory, and Anita Singh, *Household Food Security in the United States in 2017* (Washington, DC: United States Department of Agriculture, 2018), 14.

11 one estimate is an additional $10,000 a year: Greg J. Duncan and Richard J. Murnane, "Rising Inequality in Family Incomes and Children's Educational Outcomes," *RSF: The Russell Sage Foundation Journal of the Social Sciences* 2 (2) (May 2016), 142–58.

12 There was no official poverty line in America: United States Census Bureau, "Poverty: The History of a Measure," *Measuring America* (Washington, DC: United States Census Bureau, 2014).

12 there were many estimates of the number of poor: Alan Gillie, "The Origin of the Poverty Line," *Economic History Review* 49 (4) (November 1996), 715–30.

13 the SPM raised the poverty line: Fox, *Supplemental Poverty Measure: 2017*, 23.

13 The United Way Alice Project finds: Tami Luhby, "Almost Half of US Families Can't Afford Basics like Rent and Food," *CNN Business*, money.cnn.com (May 18, 2018).

13 A national survey done by Gallup every few years: Jeffrey M. Jones, "Public: Family of Four Needs to Earn Average of $52,000 to Get By," Gallup News Service (February 9, 2007).

14 But nearly 6 million children live in families: Heather Koball and Yang Jiang, *Basic Facts about Low-Income Children: Children under 18 Years, 2016* (New York: National Center for Children in Poverty, 2018), 3.

14 Nearly 20 million of all Americans live in deep poverty today: Premilla Nadasen, "Extreme Poverty Returns to America," *Washington Post*, December 21, 2017.

14 There are 3 million children: Kathryn Edin and H. Luke Shaefer, *$2.00 a Day: Living on Almost Nothing in America* (New York: Mariner Books, 2016), xvii.

15 these programs will on average amount to only 55 percent: Data used for this computation were drawn from "2018 TANF and SNAP Benefit Levels as Percentage of Federal Poverty Level (FPL)," in Ashley Burnside and Ife Floyd, *TANF Benefits Remain Low Despite Recent Increases in Some States* (Washington, DC: Center on Budget and Policy Priorities, 2019).

15 In seventeen states the total is under 50 percent: Ibid.

16 A study jsut released in 2019: Duncan and Le Menestrel, eds., *Roadmap to Reducing Child Poverty*.

17 "One of the odd aspects of the history": Michael B. Katz, *The Undeserving Poor: America's Enduring Confrontation with Poverty* (New York: Oxford University Press, 2013), 272.

18 during the regime of Margaret Thatcher: Adam Corlett, Stephen Clarke, Conor D'Arcy, and John Wood, *The Living Standards Audit 2018* (London: Resolution Foundation, 2018), 46.

18 The Trump administration has scandalously claimed: Jeff

Madrick, "That Trump Administration Claim That Poverty Is Low? Outright Flimflam," *The Nation* (October 18, 2018).

CHAPTER 2: HOW POOR CHILDREN LIVE

20 The legal scholar and Reagan adviser Edwin Meese III: David Hoffman, "Discussing Hunger in U.S., Meese Sparks a Firestorm," *Washington Post*, December 10, 1983.

21 Children who live in families with low food security: Brandi Franklin, Ashley Jones, Dejuan Love, Stephane Puckett, Justin Macklin, and Shelley White-Means, "Exploring Mediators of Food Insecurity and Obesity: A Review of Recent Literature," *Journal of Community Health* 37 (1) (February 2012), 253–64.

21 Poor prenatal nutrition is statistically related: Louise C. Ivers and Kimberly A. Cullen, "Food Insecurity: Special Considerations for Women," *American Journal of Clinical Nutrition* 94 (6) (December 2011), 1740–44S.

21 Low food security is also related to a range of adverse consequences: Katherine Alaimo, Christine M. Olson, and Edward A. Frongillo Jr., "Food Insufficiency and American School-Aged Children's Cognitive, Academic, and Psychosocial Development," *Pediatrics* 108 (1) (July 2001), 44–53, and James R. Miner, Bjorn Westgard, Travis D. Olives, Roma Patel, and Michelle Biros, "Hunger and Food Insecurity among Patients Presenting to an Urban Emergency Department," *Western Journal of Emergency Medicine* 14 (3) (May 2013), 253–62.

21 Some 44 percent of those identified as poor children: Mark Nord, *Food Insecurity in Households with Children: Prevalence, Severity, and Household Characteristics* (Washington, DC: United States Department of Agriculture, 2009), 14.

21 Food insecurity rose significantly during the Great Recession: Alisha Coleman-Jensen, William McFall, and Mark Nord, *Food Insecurity in Households with Children: Preva-*

lence, Severity, and Household Characteristics, 2010–2011 (Washington, DC: United States Department of Agriculture, 2013), 13, and Child Trends, "Percentage of Children (Ages 0–17) in Food-Insecure Households: Selected Years, 1995–2016," in "Food Insecurity," *Databank*. childtrends.org (September 17, 2018).

21 food insecurity is higher than average: Child Trends, *Food Insecurity* (Bethesda, MD: Child Trends, 2014), 4.

21 There was severe starvation and indeed death in America: Melissa Boteach, Erik Stegman, Sarah Baron, Tracey Ross, and Katie Wright, *The War on Poverty: Then and Now* (Washington, DC: Center for American Progress, 2014), 6–7.

22 Jesús de los Santos was born in the mid-1980s: Author interviews with Jesús de los Santos.

25 Most programs . . . have not sufficiently aided those further down: Hamilton Project, *Strengthening Temporary Assistance for Needy Families* (Washington, DC: Brookings Institution, 2016), 3.

25 Happily, child mortality has fallen: OECD Data, "Infant Mortality Rates: OECD Nations, 1996–2016," data.oecd .org (April 6, 2019). The United States' infant mortality rate declined from 7.3 per 1,000 live births in 1996 to 5.9 in 2016. For comparison, the Slovak Republic's infant mortality rate declined from 10.2 per 1,000 in 1996 to 5.4 in 2016.

25 Started in the late 1930s, it is now a $78-billion-a-year program: Janet Poppendieck, *Breadlines Knee-Deep in the Wheat: Food Assistance in the Great Depression* (Berkeley: University of California Press, 2014), and U.S. Department of Agriculture Food and Nutrition Service, "A Short History of SNAP," fns.usda.gov (September 17, 2018).

26 and more than 90 percent of these benefits go: Stacy Dean, *The Future of SNAP* (Washington, DC: Center on Budget and Policy Priorities, 2017).

26 children in families that participate in SNAP: Steven Carlson, Dottie Rosenbaum, Brynne Keith-Jennings, and

Catlin Nchako, *SNAP Works for America's Children* (Washington, DC: Center on Budget and Policy Priorities, 2016).

26 SNAP raised 8.4 million people out of poverty: Center on Budget and Policy Priorities, *Chart Book: SNAP Helps Struggling Families Put Food on the Table* (Washington, DC: Center on Budget and Policy Priorities, 2018), 21.

26 The average individual benefit is about $125 per person: U.S. Department of Agriculture, *Characteristics of Supplemental Nutrition Assistance Program Households: Fiscal Year 2017* (Washington, DC: United States Department of Agriculture, 2019).

26 A United Nations examination of poverty in America: United Nations Special Rapporteur, "Use of Fraud as a Smokescreen," in *Report of the Special Rapporteur on Extreme Poverty and Human Rights on His Mission to the United States of America* (New York: United Nations General Assembly, 2018), 10–11.

26 Typically, families use all their meager SNAP allowance: Elena Castellari, Chad Cotti, John Gordanier, and Orgul Ozturk, "Does the Timing of Food Stamp Distribution Matter? A Panel-Data Analysis of Monthly Purchasing Patterns of U.S. Households," *Health Economics* 26 (11) (November 2017), 1380–93.

26 usually involves low-nutrition, high-carbohydrate food: Marilyn S. Townsend, Janet Peerson, Bradley Love, Cheryl Achterberg, and Suzanne P. Murphy, "Food Insecurity Is Positively Related to Overweight in Women," *Journal of Nutrition* 131 (6) (June 2001), 1738–45.

27 "The foods that they can afford to buy": New Mexico Voices for Children, *A Health Impact Assessment of a Food Tax in New Mexico* (Albuquerque: New Mexico Voices for Children, 2015), 37.

27 The lunch program had its origins: Andrew R. Ruis, *Eating to Learn, Learning to Eat: The Origins of School Lunch in*

the United States (New Brunswick, NJ: Rutgers University Press, 2017).

28 how she managed the monthly food budget: Eli Saslow, "Too Much of Too Little: A Diet Fueled by Food Stamps Is Making South Texans Obese but Leaving Them Hungry," *Washington Post*, November 9, 2013.

29 one of the key missions of such visitors: Author interviews with Yolanda Minor.

29 A large research literature shows that hunger or poor nutrition for pregnant women: Many such studies are cited and synthesized in Ivers and Cullen, "Food Insecurity: Special Considerations for Women," 1740–44S.

30 not to ask them for a dollar: See Ajay Chaudry, *Putting Children First: How Low-Wage Working Mothers Manage Child Care* (New York: Russell Sage Foundation, 2004). Also author interview.

30 an entrepreneurial white man in Cleveland named Paul: Edin and Shaefer, *$2.00 a Day*, 111–19.

31 95 percent of those who earn between 100 and 150 percent: Jonathan Morduch and Julie Siwicki, "In and Out of Poverty: Episodic Poverty and Income Volatility in the US Financial Diaries," *Social Service Review* 91 (3) (September 2017), 390–421.

31 The source of the volatility is not only lost jobs: Ibid. See also my review essay, Jeff Madrick, "America: The Forgotten Poor," *New York Review of Books*, June 22, 2017.

32 Teenage births are sharply down among all young people: Office of Adolescent Health, "Birth Rates per 1,000 Females Ages 15–19, by Race and Hispanic Origin of Mother, 1990–2017," in *Trends in Teen Pregnancy and Childbearing* (Washington, DC: U.S. Department of Health and Human Services, 2019).

32 pregnancy among unmarried women rose sharply for all groups: Sally C. Curtin, Stephanie J. Ventura, and Gladys M. Martinez, *Recent Declines in Nonmarital Childbearing*

in the United States: National Center for Health Statistics Data Brief No. 162 (Washington, DC: U.S. Department of Health and Human Services, 2014), 1.

32 (The percentage of all births to unmarried women): National Vital Statistics Reports, *Births: Final Data for 2016* (Washington, DC: U.S. Department of Health and Human Services, 2018). See also *Births: Final Data for 2017* (Washington, DC: U.S. Department of Health and Human Services, 2019).

33 detectable cockroach allergen levels: See Virginia A. Rauh, Philip J. Landrigan, and Liz Claudio, "Housing and Health: Intersection of Poverty and Environmental Exposures," *Annals of the New York Academy of Sciences* 1136 (1) (June 2008), 276–88. See also Juan Carlos Cardet, Margee Louisias, Tonya S. King, Mario Castro, et al., "Income Is an Independent Risk Factor for Worse Asthma Outcomes," *Journal of Allergy and Clinical Immunology* 141 (2) (February 2018), 754–60.

33 "The cost-burdened share of renters doubled": Joint Center for Housing Studies of Harvard University, *The State of the Nation's Housing: 2018* (Cambridge, MA: Harvard University, 2018), 5.

33 Today, 83 percent of renters with incomes under $15,000: Joint Center for Housing Studies of Harvard University, *The State of the Nation's Housing: 2017* (Cambridge, MA: Harvard University, 2017), 31.

33 had an average of $565 left a month for all other expenses: Habitat for Humanity, *High Housing Cost Burdens in the United States* (Washington, DC: Habitat for Humanity, 2013).

33 A higher proportion of blacks and Latinos: Matthew Desmond, "Heavy Is the House: Rent Burden among the American Urban Poor," *International Journal of Urban and Regional Research* 42 (1) (January 2018), 160–70.

33 "A similar proportion of low-income homeowners and

renters": Laurie Goodman and Bhargavi Ganesh, "Low-Income Homeowners Are as Burdened by Housing Costs as Renters," *Urban Wire: The Blog of the Urban Institute* (June 14, 2017).

34 "the majority of poor renting families": Desmond, "Heavy Is the House" 160.

34 Too often the poor are relegated to the worst quality of housing: Amy Edmonds, Paula Braveman, Elaine Arkin, and Doug Jutte, *How Do Neighborhood Conditions Shape Health?* (Princeton, NJ: Robert Wood Johnson Foundation, 2015).

34 They also must live in overcrowded quarters: Claudia D. Solari and Robert D. Mare, "Housing Crowding Effects on Children's Wellbeing," *Social Science Research* 41 (2) (March 2012), 464–76.

34 frequent moving is damaging: Kathleen M. Ziol-Guest and Claire C. McKenna, "Early Childhood Housing Instability and School Readiness," *Child Development* 85 (1) (January–February 2014), 103–13; Megan Sandel, Richard Sheward, Stephanie Ettinger de Cuba, Sharon M. Coleman, et al., "Unstable Housing and Caregiver and Child Health in Renter Families,"*Pediatrics* 141 (2) (February 2018), 1–12; and HUD Office of Policy Development and Research (PD&R), "How Housing Instability Impacts Individual and Family Well-Being," *PD&R Edge*, November 2018.

34 housing subsidies, in turn, improve child outcomes: Mary Cunningham and Graham McDonald, "Housing as a Platform for Improving Education Outcomes among Low-Income Children," *What Works Collaborative* (Washington, DC: Urban Institute, 2012), 1–16.

34 elevated levels of lead in their blood: Yutaka Aoki1 and Debra J. Brody, "WIC Participation and Blood Lead Levels among Children 1–5, Years: 2007–2014," *Environmental Health Perspectives* 126(6) (June 2018), 1–6.

35 legal evictions of the poor are rising rapidly: Matthew

Desmond, *Evicted: Poverty and Profit in the American City* (New York: Broadway Books, 2016).

35 he has found cities with twice, even four times, that rate: Matthew Desmond, Lavar Edmonds, Ashley Gromis, et al., "Top Evicting Large Cities in America," *Eviction Lab* (2018).

35 "The sound of eviction court was a soft hum": Desmond, *Evicted*, 97.

36 2.3 million people received an eviction notice: Matthew Desmond and Colin Kinniburgh, "The Faces of Eviction," *Dissent* (Fall 2018), 33–41.

36 Thirty-three percent of homeless people today are families with children: Meghan Henry, Rian Watt, Lily Rosenthal, and Azim Shivji, *2017 Annual Homeless Assessment Report to Congress* (Washington, DC: U.S. Department of Housing and Urban Development, 2017), 1.

36 2.5 million children will be homeless in America: Family Promise, *Homelessness & Poverty Fact Sheet* (Summit, NJ: Family Promise, 2019).

36 Some one in seven children in New York City public primary schools: Institute for Children, Poverty & Homelessness, *On the Map: The Atlas of Student Homelessness in New York City 2017* (New York: Institute for Children, Poverty & Homelessness, 2017).

37 homeless children are twice as likely to experience hunger: National Center on Family Homelessness, *The Characteristics and Needs of Families Experiencing Homelessness* (Washington, DC: American Institutes for Research, 2008), 5.

37 One out of three homeless children are separated from their families: Douglas Walton, Michelle Wood, and Lauren Dunton, *Child Separation among Families Experiencing Homelessness* (Washington, DC: U.S. Department of Health and Human Services, 2018).

37 homeless children pay a price in poor health: Linda J. Anooshian, "Violence and Aggression in the Lives of

Homeless Children: A Review," *Aggression and Violent Behavior* 10 (2005), 129–52.

37 "Every day is a different day with Mark": Author interview with Lauren.

37 Brianna is now a well-paid social worker: Author interview with Brianna.

38 In Lake County, Tennessee, 46 percent of children live in poverty: "Tennessee: Children in Poverty," *County Health Rankings & Roadmaps* (Princeton, NJ: Robert Wood Johnson Foundation and University of Wisconsin Population Health Institute, 2019).

38 "Some take only women with children under age five": Edin and Shaefer, *$2.00 a Day*, 104.

39 has not made the contemporary age of personal responsibility easy: Ajay Chaudry, Juan Manuel Perdoza, Heather Sandtrom, Anna Danziger, et al., "Child Care Choices of Working Families" (Washington, DC: Urban Institute, 2011).

39 Part of the solution is emerging in New York City: See National Institute for Early Education Research and CityHealth, *Pre-K in American Cities* (Bethesda, MD: de Beaumont Foundation, 2019). The authors of this study conclude:

> New York City's Pre-K services for 4-year-olds increase identification of health and physical concerns, which results in earlier remedies. Adults who have attended Pre-K are far more likely to have improved health behaviors and better health, which lowers health care costs. However, progress toward attaining widespread provision of high-quality Pre-K is slow.
>
> Two cities stand out as exemplars for providing funding to allow all children to attend Pre-K programs: Washington, D.C., serves almost the entire population of 3- and

4-year-olds, and New York City serves almost all 4-year-olds and is scaling up to serve all 3-year-olds. Because of accessible state-funded Pre-K services at the state level in Florida, Georgia, and Oklahoma, programs in Jacksonville, Atlanta, and Tulsa serve most 4-year-olds. Other cities such as Seattle, Columbus, and Philadelphia have a plan to scale to full access by targeting low-income children first.

40–41 the likelihood of poor mothers giving birth to a low-birth-weight child: Melissa L. Martinson and Nancy E. Reichman, "Socioeconomic Inequalities in Low Birth Weight in the United States, the United Kingdom, Canada, and Australia," *American Journal of Public Health* 106 (4) (April 2016), 748–54.

41 The low-birth-weight rate for black mothers: Katelyn Newman, "Report: Pattern of Racial Disparity in Low Birthweight in U.S.," *U.S. News & World Report* (March 14, 2018). See also *County Health Rankings & Roadmaps* (Princeton, NJ: Robert Wood Johnson Foundation and University of Wisconsin Population Health Institute, 2019).

41 Chris Rogers's story was closely followed: Children's Defense Fund, *America's Cradle to Prison Pipeline* (Washington, DC: Children's Defense Fund, 2005), 109.

42 now have insurance for at least part of the year: Child Trends, *Health Care Coverage for Children* (Bethesda, MD: Child Trends, 2018), 1.

44 Its rate of child poverty is now more than 46 percent: Lucy May, "New Census Data Show Child Poverty on the Rise in Cincinnati, Hamilton County," *WCPO Cincinnati*, WCPO.com (September 13, 2018).

45 By density, America's West and South remain the poorest regions: Joseph Dalaker, *Poverty in the United States in 2017*, 7.

45 He found that poverty concentration started to rise rap-

idly: Paul Jargowsky, "The Architecture of Segregation," *Century Foundation: Race & Inequality* (August 7, 2015). See also "New Data Reveals Huge Increases in Concentrated Poverty Since 2000," ibid. (August 9, 2015).

46 such segregated and poor neighborhoods severely compound the disadvantages: See Wilson's hugely influential *The Truly Disadvantaged: The Inner City, the Underclass, and Public Policy* (Chicago: University of Chicago Press, 1987).

46 A higher percentage of both black and Latino children live in high-poverty neighborhoods: National Low Income Housing Coalition, "Population Living in High-Poverty Neighborhoods Almost Doubles since 2000," nlihc.org (August 17, 2015).

46 The rise in high-poverty neighborhoods has been greatest in smaller metro areas: Ibid. See Jargowsky, "Architecture of Segregation."

CHAPTER 3: AMERICAN ATTITUDES TOWARD POVERTY

49 American wages were virtually always higher: See, for example, *Bulletin of the Department of Labor, No. 18—September 1898* (Washington, DC: U.S. Department of Labor, 1898), 668. In 1881, according to this 1898 bulletin, average daily wages in Great Britain were $1.37; in Paris, $1.22; in Liege, Belgium, 63¢—and in the United States, $2.40. This huge wage differential was reported all the way though the 1870–98 period surveyed in this publication.

50 "industrial capitalism, urbanization, greater poverty": Walter I. Trattner, *Poor Law to Welfare State: A History of Social Welfare in America* (New York: Free Press, 2007), 52.

50 "No man who is temperate, frugal, and willing to work need suffer": Ibid., 54.

51 A pioneering psychologist, G. Stanley Hall, studied the development of the child: Granville Stanley Hall, *Adolescence: Its Psychology and Its Relations to Physiology, Anthropology, Sociology, Sex, Crime, Religion and Education* (New

York: Appleton, 1904). See also Lorine Pruette, *G. Stanley Hall, A Biography of a Mind* (New York: Appleton, 1926), and Dorothy Ross, *G. Stanley Hall: The Psychologist as Prophet* (Chicago: University of Chicago Press, 1972).

52 some 14 million between 1860 and 1900: Paul Spickard, *Almost All Aliens: Immigration, Race, and Colonialism in American History* (New York: Routledge, 2009), 235.

52 "Many, many thousand families receive wages so inadequate": Robert Hunter, *Poverty* (New York: Macmillan, 1904), 47.

53 In 1912, a group of settlement house workers compiled a list of requirements: Mike Wallace, *Greater Gotham: A History of New York City from 1898 to 1919* (New York: Oxford University Press, 2017), 578–79.

53 "the new party has become the American exponent": Ibid.

54 Franklin Roosevelt was a small-government advocate: See Arthur M. Schlesinger Jr., *The Age of Roosevelt*, vol. 1: *The Crisis of the Old Order, 1919–1933*; vol. 2: *The Coming of the New Deal, 1933–1935*; vol. 3: *The Politics of Upheaval, 1935–1936* (New York: Houghton Mifflin, 1957; 1958; 1960).

54 In 1933, only 5 percent of CCC workers were black: Harvard Sitkoff, *A New Deal for Blacks: The Emergence of Civil Rights as a National Issue; The Depression Decade* (New York: Oxford University Press, 1978), 39.

55 Robert Fechner, the head of the CCC: John C. Paige, *The Civilian Conservation Corps and the National Park Service, 1933–1942: An Administrative History* (Washington, DC: National Parks Service, 1985), 93–94.

55 segregation was the norm in most federally funded programs: Ira Katznelson, *When Affirmative Action Was White: An Untold History of Racial Inequality in Twentieth-Century America* (New York: W. W. Norton, 2005), 140.

55 Mortgages to blacks: Richard Rothstein, *The Color of Law: A Forgotten History of How Our Government Segregated America* (New York: Liveright, 2017).

55 Strong lobbying pressure: *November 19, 1945: President*

Truman's Proposed Health Program (Independence, MO: Harry S. Truman Presidential Library, 2006).

55 under Republican Dwight Eisenhower, social programs were expanded modestly: Andrew Glass, "Eisenhower Approves Expanded Social Security Coverage, Sept. 1, 1954," *Politico* (September 1, 2018).

55 but it was sold to the public as a national security program: Tom Lewis, *Divided Highways: Building the Interstate Highways, Transforming American Life* (New York: Viking, 1997).

56 "almost everybody has assumed that because of the New Deal's social legislation": Dwight Macdonald, "Our Invisible Poor," *New Yorker*, January 11, 1963.

58 The Harvard economist John Kenneth Galbraith: John Kenneth Galbraith, *The Affluent Society* (New York: Houghton Mifflin, 1958).

59 Galbraith's "one family in thirteen": Ibid., 252.

60 Johnson, mindful of conservative views: Gareth Davies, "War on Dependency: Liberal Individualism and the Economic Opportunity Act of 1964," *Journal of American Studies* 26 (2) (August 1992), 205–31.

60 The War on Poverty included Head Start, the Job Corps: Martha J. Bailey and Nicole J. Duquette, "How Johnson Fought the War on Poverty: The Economics and Politics of Funding at the Office of Economic Opportunity," *Journal of Economic History* 74 (2) (June 2014), 351–88.

60 Johnson also made food stamps permanent by law: U.S. Department of Agriculture Food and Nutrition Service, "Short History of SNAP," 2.

60 In them, he expanded Social Security benefits: Irving Bernstein, *Guns or Butter: The Presidency of Lyndon Johnson* (New York: Oxford University Press, 1996).

61 Aid to Families with Dependent Children (AFDC) . . . was sharply expanded in the 1960s: Jill Quadagno, *The Color of Welfare: How Racism Undermined the War on Poverty* (New York: Oxford University Press, 1994), 119–21.

61 Sargent Shriver argued that the country should set a goal: Indivar Dutta-Gupta, *The Unfinished War on Poverty* (Washington, DC: Center on Budget and Policy Priorities, 2012).

61 based on the work of a dedicated analyst . . . Mollie Orshansky: Gordon M. Fisher, *The Development of the Orshansky Poverty Thresholds and Their Subsequent History as the Official U.S. Poverty Measure* (Washington, DC: United States Census Bureau, 1997).

62 an absolute line would also make it possible to give the appearance of reducing poverty quickly: Alice O'Connor, *Poverty Knowledge: Social Science, Social Policy, and the Poor in Twentieth Century U.S. History* (Princeton, NJ: Princeton University Press, 2001), 154.

62 Orshansky's poverty line was proposed in a report in 1963: Fisher, *Development of the Orshansky Poverty Thresholds*, 6. See Mollie Orshansky, "Children of the Poor," *Social Security Bulletin* 26 (7) (July 1963), 3–13, and "Counting the Poor: Another Look at the Poverty Profile," *Social Security Bulletin* 28 (1) (January 1965), 3–29.

63 noted that levels were increased substantially every decade or two: Oscar Ornati, *Poverty Amid Affluence: A Report on a Research Project Carried Out at the New School for Social Research* (New York: Twentieth Century Fund, 1966).

64 "As the general level of living moves upward and expands": Orshansky, "Children of the Poor," 3.

64 "The difficulties in setting the poverty line are increased": Mollie Orshansky, "Recounting the Poor—A Five-Year Review," *Social Security Bulletin* 29 (4) (April 1966), 20–37, 22.

64 "Measures of income adequacy (or of poverty) change over time": Robert Ball, *Memorandum to Wilbur J. Cohen, Under Secretary of Health, Education, and Welfare; Subject: Poverty Research—Your Memorandum of October 29* (Washington, DC: Social Security Administration, 1965). Quoted in Fisher, *Development of the Orshansky Poverty Thresholds*, 9.

64 "It is easy to observe that poverty in the U.S. today": Ibid., 33.

65 the federal government spent $168 billion: Robert E. Wood, *From Marshall Plan to Debt Crisis: Foreign Aid and Development Choices in the World Economy* (Berkeley: University of California Press, 1986), 197.

66 When adopted, the OPM was about 50 percent of typical family incomes: National Center for Children in Poverty, "Researchers, Analysts Say Updated Poverty Gauge Long Overdue: Measurement Formula Unchanged Since 1960s," nccp.org (April 30, 2008).

68 when the supplemental measure was officially published: Fox, *Supplemental Poverty Measure: 2017*, 1.

68 The national supplemental poverty income threshold: Ibid., 23.

CHAPTER 4: THE ANTI-WELFARE POLICY CONSENSUS

71 TANF eventually covered only one-third as many families: Child Trends, *Child Recipients of Welfare (AFDC/TANF): Indicators on Children and Youth* (Bethesda, MD: Child Trends, 2014), 2.

71 The Earned Income Tax Credit, originally a Republican program: Thomas L. Hungerford and Rebecca Thiess, *The Earned Income Tax Credit and the Child Tax Credit: History, Purpose, Goals, and Effectiveness* (Washington, DC: Economic Policy Institute, 2015).

71 Congressman Ro Khanna, for example, has proposed doubling benefits: Chuck Marr, Emily Horton, and Brendan Duke, *Brown-Khanna Proposal to Expand EITC Would Raise Incomes of 47 Million Working Households* (Washington, DC: Center on Budget and Policy Priorities, 2017).

71 This tax expenditure . . . now provides more than $60 billion in benefits: Heather Hahn, "Surprising Tax Fact: More Than One-Third of Federal Support for Children Comes

through Tax Provisions," *Urban Wire: The Blog of the Urban Institute* (April 15, 2019).

72 declined in cost from a high of $26 billion: Office of Human Services Policy, *Aid to Families with Dependent Children: The Baseline* (Washington, DC: U.S. Department of Health and Human Services, 1998), 63.

72 In 2017, about 44 percent of families with children received benefits from the EITC: Hilary Hoynes, Jesse Rothstein, and Krista Ruffini, *Making Work Pay Better through an Expanded Earned Income Tax Credit* (Washington, DC: Hamilton Project and Brookings Institution, 2017), 4.

72 The benefits diminish gradually at higher incomes: Gene Falk and Margot L. Crandall-Hollick, *The Earned Income Tax Credit (EITC): An Overview* (Washington, DC: Congressional Research Service, 2018), 5.

72 Together these programs have raised 8.9 million people above the supplemental poverty line:, *Policy Basics: The Child Tax Credit* (Washington, DC: Center on Budget and Policy Priorities, 2019).

72 It is a $2,000 tax credit per child: Internal Revenue Service, *Get Ready for Taxes: Here's How the New Tax Law Revised Family Tax Credits* (Washington, DC: Internal Revenue Service, 2018).

72–73 previously, the tax credit had started to phase out at $75,000 for single filers: Ibid.

73 In 2017, the program cost the federal government about $50 billion: Hoynes and Schanzenbach, "Safety Net Investments in Children," 5.

73 in 2018, $104 billion: Erica York, "Family Provisions in the New Tax Code," *Tax Foundation Fiscal Fact* 621 (October 2018), 5.

73 A single parent with two children: Internal Revenue Service, *Earned Income Credit: For Use in Preparing 2018 Returns* (Washington, DC: Internal Revenue Service, 2019).

73 "welfare reform and the decline in unconditional cash

assistance": Hoynes and Schanzenbach, "Safety Net Investments in Children," 29.

74 In total, federal spending on children: Julia B. Isaacs, Cary Lou, Heather Hahn, Ashley Hong, Caleb Quakenbush, and G. Eugene Steuerle, *Kids' Share 2018: Report on Federal Expenditures on Children through 2017 and Future Projections* (Washington, DC: Urban Institute, 2018), 10.

74 In 1990, all such programs for children: Data used for this computation were drawn from "Trends in Outlays on Children as a Share of Total Budget Outlays," in Julia B. Isaacs, Stephanie Rennane, Tracy Vericker, et al., *Kids' Share 2011: Report on Federal Expenditures on Children through 2010* (Washington, DC: Urban Institute, 2011), 18.

75 all federal spending on children . . . has remained: Ibid., 41.

75 federal spending on the elderly grew to 7.1 percent: Data used for this computation were drawn from Louis Jacobson, "Federal Spending on Old and Young, By the Numbers," *Politifact*, January 28, 2013.

75 and is more than 9.3 percent of GDP today: Hoynes and Schanzenbach, "Safety Net Investments in Children," 3.

75 "federal spending on the elderly between 1960 and 2017 increased": Isaacs et al., *Kids' Share 2018*, 34.

75 overall spending on the elderly per person in America: Julia B. Isaacs, *Spending on Children and the Elderly* (Washington, DC: Brookings Institution, 2009), 1.

76 Some $1.7 trillion in tax revenues is forgone annually: Data used for this computation were drawn from Uwe Reinhardt, "Revenue Loss from Select Tax Expenditures," in Uwe Reinhardt, *Modeling Tax Deductibility as Ad Valorem Subsidies*, paper presented at Princeton University, Scholar .princeton.edu (Fall 2014).

76 fell from 87 percent of social spending in 1990: Hoynes and Schanzenbach, "Safety Net Investments in Children," 26.

76 "In 1992, welfare reform has not yet occurred:" Ibid., 27.

77 "there have been substantial shifts over the past 20 years": Ibid., 3.

78 Ronald Reagan's 1983 comment: Francis X. Clines, "President Denies Blame for Deficit," *New York Times*, October 8, 1983.

78 The official poverty rate . . . was 22.4 percent in 1959: Sheldon Danziger, Koji Chavez, and Erin Cumberworth, *Poverty and the Great Recession* (New York and Stanford, CA: Russell Sage Foundation and Stanford Center on Poverty and Inequality, 2012), 1.

78 Child poverty rates under the non-official SPM: Ibid., 3. See also Chad Stone, Danilo Trisi, Arloc Sherman, and Roderick Taylor, *A Guide to Statistics on Historical Trends in Income Inequality* (Washington, DC: Center on Budget and Policy Priorities, 2018).

79 The Field Foundation . . . had sent medical observers to the Deep South: Marian Wright Edelman, "The Continuing Scourge of Poverty, Hunger and Hopelessness in Rich America," *Children's Defense Fund: Child Watch Column* (April 11, 2017).

79 a CBS television documentary showed a newborn die of malnutrition: David Martin Davies, "'Hunger in America': The 1968 Documentary That Exposed San Antonio Poverty," Texas Public Radio, TPR.org (June 8, 2018).

79 "It is not possible any more to find very easily the bloated bellies": Michael B. Katz, *In The Shadow of the Poorhouse: A Social History of Welfare in America* (New York: Basic Books, 1996), 275.

80 Originally, participants had to buy food stamps: Robert Greenstein, *Commentary: SNAP's Bipartisan Legacy Can Serve as a Model* (Washington, DC: Center on Budget and Policy Priorities, 2017), 2.

CHAPTER 5: THE "CULTURE OF POVERTY"

82 Oscar Lewis, writing about Mexico, Puerto Rico: See Oscar Lewis, *Five Families: Mexican Case Studies in the Culture of Poverty* (New York: Basic Books, 1959), and *La*

Vida: A Puerto Rican Family in the Culture of Poverty—San Juan and New York (New York: Random House, 1966).

82 "The appeal of the 'culture of poverty' is that it offers a clear explanation": Mark Gould, Kaaryn Gustafson, and Mario Luis Small, "Re-Evaluating the 'Culture of Poverty': Roundtable," in Stephen Suh and Kia Heise, eds., *The Society Pages* (October 14, 2014). See also Kaaryn Gustafson, *Cheating Welfare: Public Assistance and the Criminalization of Poverty* (New York: NYU Press, 2012).

83 "The myth of otherness associated with being poor in America": Alice O'Connor, quoted in "Hedgehog Review's Fall Issue Ponders How We Think about the Poor," *UVAToday*, November 7, 2014.

83 he asserted that ghetto life is "utterly different": Ken Auletta, *The Underclass* (New York: Random House, 1982).

83 "As apart as all of black life is, ghetto life is a thousand times more so": Nicholas Lemann, "The Origins of the Underclass," *The Atlantic* (July 1986).

84 "Members of the underclass don't share traditional values": Quoted in William Julius Wilson, "The American Underclass: Inner-City Ghettos and the Norms of Citizenship," lecture delivered at Harvard University (Cambridge, MA: April 26, 1988).

85 "poverty and welfare were both 'transitory' conditions": O'Connor, *Poverty Knowledge*, 252.

85 found that few of the poor were embedded long-term in poverty: See Greg Duncan, *Years of Poverty, Years of Plenty—The Changing Economic Fortunes of American Workers and Families* (Ann Arbor: Institute for Social Research at the University of Michigan, 1984).

85 they accounted for a majority of the costs of the existing welfare system: Mary Jo Bane and David T. Ellwood, "Slipping Into and Out of Poverty: The Dynamics of Spells," *National Bureau of Economic Research Working Paper* 1199 (September 1983), and *Journal of Human Resources* 21 (1) (Winter 1986), 1–23.

86 "The consequences of 'culture of poverty' arguments have been disastrous": Mark Gould, Kaaryn Gustafson, and Mario Luis Small, "Re-Evaluating the 'Culture of Poverty': Roundtable," 5–6.

87 Moynihan had given the argument about black culture its forward spin: See Godfrey Hodgson, *The Gentleman from New York: Daniel Patrick Moynihan; A Biography* (New York: Houghton Mifflin Harcourt, 2000) and Stephen Hess, *The Professor and the President: Daniel Patrick Moynihan in the Nixon White House* (Washington, DC: Brookings Institution Press, 2014).

87 wrote about the "tangle of pathology" of the black family: Daniel Patrick Moynihan, *The Negro Family: The Case for National Action* (Washington, DC: Office of Policy Planning and Research and United States Department of Labor, 1965).

87 "three centuries of injustice": Ibid., 1.

89 "strengthening the Negro family": Ibid., 32.

89 Simple facts do not support the family dissolution thesis: See Herbert Gutman, *The Black Family in Slavery and Freedom, 1750–1925* (New York: Pantheon, 1976).

89 The sociologist Herbert Gans wrote that the matriarchal family "has not yet been proven pathological": Quoted in O'Connor, *Poverty Knowledge*, 208.

90 Nearly three-quarters of all births to black women: Brooklynn K. Hitchens and Yasser Arafat Payne, "'Brenda's Got a Baby': Black Single Motherhood and Street Life as a Site of Resilience in Wilmington, Delaware," *Journal of Black Psychology* 43 (1) (January 2017), 50–76, 52.

90 headed by a female without a spouse: Ibid.

90 For black women, the proportion roughly flattened out from 1990 forward: Child Trends, *Births to Unmarried Women* (Bethesda, MD: Child Trends, 2018), 1.

90 A powerful welfare rights movement urged them to sign up: See Premilla Nadasen, *Welfare Warriors: The Welfare Rights Movement in the United States* (New York: Rout-

ledge, 2004); Felicia Kornbluh, *The Battle for Welfare Rights: Politics and Poverty in Modern America* (Philadelphia: University of Pennsylvania Press, 2007); and Larry R. Jackson and William Arthur Johnson, *Protest by the Poor: The Welfare Rights Movement in New York City* (Lexington, MA: Lexington Books, 1974).

91 the most unpopular social policy of the 1980s: Steven V. Roberts, "Food Stamps Program: How It Grew and How Reagan Wants to Cut It Back," *New York Times*, April 4, 1981.

91 "can only get SNAP for 3 months in 3 years": U.S. Department of Agriculture Food and Nutrition Service, "Able-Bodied Adults Without Dependents (ABAWDs)."

92 the drastic decline in the AFDC-TANF program: Robert A. Moffitt, "The Deserving Poor, the Family, and the U.S. Welfare System," *Demography* 52 (3) (June 2015), 729–49, 741.

93 In 2015, TANF spending came to just 0.54 percent of total federal outlays: Melissa Kearney, "Welfare and the Federal Budget," *Econofact*, July 25, 2017.

93 Only 23 percent of poor families received TANF in 2015: Nisha G. Patel, "Strengthening the TANF Program: Putting Children at the Center and Increasing Access to Good Jobs for Parents." Testimony before the Subcommittee on Human Resources, Committee on Ways and Means (Washington, DC: United States House of Representatives, May 9, 2018), 6.

93 In fourteen states, only 10 percent: Ife Floyd, *Trump's TANF Cuts Would Hurt the Poorest Families, and States Might Make Them Worse* (Washington, DC: Center on Budget and Policy Priorities, 2017).

93 And those benefits under the original welfare program: Ife Floyd and Liz Schott, *TANF Benefits Fell Further in 2011 and Are Worth Much Less than in 1996 in Most States* (Washington, DC: Center on Budget and Policy Priorities, 2011), 1.

94 no higher than 60 percent of the official poverty line: Ashley Burnside and Ife Floyd, *TANF Benefits Remain Low Despite Recent Increases in Some States*, 1.

94 On average, a three-person family who qualify: *Chart Book: Temporary Assistance for Needy Families* (Washington, DC: Center on Budget and Policy Priorities, 2018), 6.

94 Adding SNAP and TANF together: Burnside and Floyd, *TANF Benefits Remain Low*, 1.

95 Americans have a "negative view of the poor": Max Rose and Frank R. Baumgartner, "Framing the Poor: Media Coverage and U.S. Poverty Policy, 1960–2008," *Policy Studies Journal* 41 (1) (February 2013), 22–53, 42.

95 70.1 percent of French respondents included "injustice in society": Dorota Lepianka, John Gelissen, and Wim van Oorschot, "Popular Explanations of Poverty in Europe: Effects of Contextual and Individual Characteristics across 28 European Countries," *Acta Sociologica* 53 (1) (March 2010), 53–72, 63.

CHAPTER 6: RACISM AND POVERTY

97 "Celtic ape-men with sloping foreheads": Christopher Klein, "When America Despised the Irish: The 19th Century's Refugee Crisis," History.com (March 14, 2019).

98 the widely distributed Dorothea Lange photographs: See Milton Metlzer, *Dorothea Lange: A Photographer's Life* (Syracuse, NY: Syracuse University Press, 2000), and Judith Keller, *In Focus: Dorothea Lange—Photographs from the J. Paul Getty Museum* (Los Angeles: Getty Publications, 2002).

98 mentioned black poverty just once: Isaac Max Rubinow, *The Quest for Security* (New York: Henry Holt, 1934), 161.

99 Presidents Kennedy and Johnson both signed: Jackie Mansky, "The Origins of the Term 'Affirmative Action,'" *Smithsonian* magazine, Smithsonian.com (June 22, 2016).

99–100 "In 1966, the country saw 43 race riots": Richard D. Kahlenberg, "The Inclusive Populism of Robert F. Kennedy," *Century Foundation: Democracy* (March 16, 2018).

100 "For several decades, Americans ha[d] voted basically along the lines of property": Richard M. Scammon and Ben J. Wattenberg, *The Real Majority: An Extraordinary Examination of the American Electorate* (New York: Coward, McCann & Geoghegan, 1970), 20 and 39.

100 a dramatic formal demand for economic equality: See Sylvie Laurent, *King and the Other America: The Poor People's Campaign and the Quest for Economic Equality* (Berkeley: University of California Press, 2018).

101 "The more Negroes who register as Democrats in the South": James Boyd, "Nixon's Southern Strategy: 'It's All in the Charts,'" *New York Times*, May 17, 1970.

101 Forty-two percent of the poor are white: Alan Berube, *The Continuing Evolution of American Poverty and Its Implications for Community Development* (Washington, DC: Brookings Institution, 2016), 61.

101 Nearly one-third of black children are poor: *Child Poverty in America 2017: National Analysis* (Washington, DC: Children's Defense Fund, 2018), 1.

102 Eight percent of all children live in families whose incomes are half: Child Trends, "Key Facts About Child Poverty," *Children in Poverty* (January 28, 2019).

103 About 2.1 million of these are children under age five: *Supporting Young Children: Addressing Poverty, Promoting Opportunity, and Advancing Equity in Policy* (Washington, DC: Center for the Study of Social Policy, 2018), 2.

103 About 15 percent of black children and 10 percent of Hispanic children live in deep poverty: Child Trends, "Key Facts About Child Poverty," 3.

103 In 2010, whites made up 64 percent of the population: Arloc Sherman, Robert Greenstein, and Kathy Ruffing, *Contrary to "Entitlement Society" Rhetoric, Over Nine-Tenths*

of Entitlement Benefits Go to Elderly, Disabled, or Working Households (Washington, DC: Center on Budget and Policy Priorities, 2012).

103 "Of all the people who are poor in this country": Martin Gilens, *Why Americans Hate Welfare: Race, Media, and the Politics of Antipoverty Policy* (Chicago: University of Chicago Press, 1999), 68.

104 "thirty addresses, twelve Social Security cards": Quoted in David Zucchino, *Myth of the Welfare Queen: A Pulitzer Prize–winning Journalist's Portrait of Women on the Line* (New York: Scribner, 1997), 65.

104 But only 15 percent of the apartments had such ceilings: "'Welfare Queen' Becomes Issue in Reagan Campaign," *New York Times*, February 15, 1976.

105 an ideological screed: George Gilder, *Wealth and Poverty* (New York: Basic Books, 1981).

106 Still more influential was the best seller *Losing Ground*: Charles Murray, *Losing Ground: American Social Policy, 1950–1980* (New York: Basic Books, 1984).

107 the value of the government programs adjusted for inflation: U.S. Department of Health and Human Services, "Trends in AFDC and Food Stamp Benefits, 1972–1994," *ASPE Research Notes* (May 1995), 1–5.

107 the book argued ... that blacks had innately inferior IQs: Charles Murray and Richard Herrnstein, *The Bell Curve: Intelligence and Class Structure in American Life* (New York: Free Press, 1994).

108 "It has been more difficult to assemble data": Ibid., 289.

108 "You cannot imagine it because that kind of thing cannot be said": Charles Murray, "Deeper into the Brain," *National Review*, January 24, 2000.

109 "Even if only half or one quarter of this book endures the assault": Quoted in Jonathan Tilove, "Charles Murray's 'Bell Curve' Reveals Republican Fissures on Race," Newhouse News Service, January 29, 1995.

110 Although the percentage of families receiving AFDC tripled: Gilens, *Why Americans Hate Welfare*, 18–19.

110 Average monthly SNAP benefits in the mid-1990s were roughly $70 per person: Office of Human Services Policy, *Aid to Families with Dependent Children: The Baseline*, 126.

110 60 to 70 percent believed America was spending too much on welfare: Gilens, *Why Americans Hate Welfare*, 28.

110 "racial attitudes have a profound impact on opposition to welfare": Ibid., 5.

110 He analyzed the media representation of the poor: Ibid., 111.

111 After being ignored for so long: Ibid., 113.

111 a moderate "whitening of poverty images": Ibid., 122.

111 blacks were the focus of 57 percent of stories about poverty: Ibid., 146.

112 unemployment was one of the three most important issues in the nation: Ibid., 136.

112 "'lack of effort on their own part'": Ibid., 139.

112 The scholar Bas van Doorn updated Martin Gilens's findings: Bas W. van Doorn, "Pre- and Post-Welfare Reform Media Portrayals of Poverty in the United States: The Continuing Importance of Race and Ethnicity," *Politics & Policy* 43 (1) (February 2015), 142–62.

113 As Richard Rothstein summarizes: See endnote 13 to chapter 3, "American Attitudes toward Poverty."

113 The historian and political scientist Ira Katznelson *When Affirmative Action Was White*: See endnote 12 to chapter 3, "American Attitudes toward Poverty."

114 Declining real wages for lower-income Americans: National Employment Law Project, *Occupational Wage Declines Since the Great Recession* (New York: National Employment Law Project, 2015).

CHAPTER 7: HARDSHIP AND POVERTY

115 "Updating the statistical measure of poverty would tend to change our view": Denton R. Vaughan, *Exploring the Use of*

the Views of the Public to Set Income Poverty Thresholds and Adjust Them over Time (Washington, DC: United States Census Bureau, 2004), 33.

116 In 2017, 8 percent of children—almost 6 million: Data used for this computation were drawn from Child Trends, "Key Facts about Child Poverty," *Children in Poverty* (January 28, 2019) and "Child Population by Age Group in the United States," *Kids Count Data Center* (Baltimore: Annie E. Casey Foundation, 2018).

116 4.8 percent of children are in deep poverty under the SPM: Fox, *Supplemental Poverty Measure: 2017*, 7.

116 the typical (median) poor child in America: *Measuring Child Poverty: New League Tables of Child Poverty in the World's Rich Countries, Report Card 10* (Florence, Italy: UNICEF Innocenti Research Centre, 2012), 14.

117 There may have been 1.5 million families whose members live on $2 a day: Shaefer, *$2.00 a Day*, xvii.

117 "If the safety net had remained as effective": Arloc Sherman and Danilo Trisi, *Safety Net for Poorest Weakened after Welfare Law but Regained Strength in Great Recession, at Least Temporarily: A Decade after Welfare Overhaul, More Children in Deep Poverty* (Washington, DC: Center on Budget and Policy Priorities, 2015), 1.

118 and eliminated for most legal immigrants: U.S. Department of Agriculture Food and Nutrition Service, "Short History of SNAP," 8.

118 A study of families with children in New York City is especially alarming: Christopher Wimer, Sophie Collyer, Irwin Garfinkel, Matthew Maury, Kathryn Neckerman, et al., *The Persistence of Disadvantage in New York City: A Three-Year Perspective from the Poverty Tracker* (New York: Columbia Population Research Center, 2016).

118 Nearly three out of four low-income New Yorkers: Apurva Mehrotra and Nancy Rankin, *The Unheard Third: 2011* (New York: Community Service Society, 2012), 4.

120 Some prominent scholars once rejected the relationship:

Cf. Ajay Chaudry and Christopher Wimer, "Poverty is Not Just an Indicator: The Relationship Between Income, Poverty, and Child Well-Being," *Academic Pediatrics* 16 (3S) (April 2016), S23–S29.

120 A survey of material deprivation: Romina Boarini and Marco Mira d'Ercole, *Measures of Material Deprivation in OECD Countries* (Paris: OECD, 2006).

120 In 2015, 43.5 percent of children living below the official poverty line: Child Trends, "Percentage of Children (Ages 0–17) in Food-Insecure Households: Selected Years, 1995–2016."

121 Of those whose family incomes are up to 1.3 times: Coleman-Jensen, Rabbitt, Gregory, and Singh, *Household Food Security in the United States in 2017*, 14.

121 About 1 percent of all families with children under eighteen: Child Trends, *Food Insecurity* (September 17, 2018), 1.

121 "Household food insecurity has insidious effects": Maureen Black, "Household Food Insecurities: Threats to Children's Well-Being," *The SES Indicator, American Psychological Association* (June 2012), 1–5.

121 Children know far fewer words: Cf. Anya Kamenetz, "Let's Stop Talking about the '30 Million Word Gap,'" *All Things Considered,* NPR.org (June 1, 2018).

122 poor children were 1.3 times more likely to have a learning disability: Jeanne Brooks-Gunn and Greg J. Duncan, "The Effects of Poverty on Children," *The Future of Children* 7 (2) (Summer-Autumn 1997), 55–71.

122 that IQ was reduced between 6 and 13 percentage points: Ibid.

123 The neurological research is built on a hypothesis: Sara B. Johnson, Anne W. Riley, Douglas A. Granger, and Jenna Riis, "The Science of Early Life Toxic Stress for Pediatric Practice and Advocacy," *Pediatrics* 131 (2) (February 2013), 319–27.

123 "recurrent physical and/or emotional abuse": Jack P.

Shonkoff, W. Thomas Boyce, and Bruce S. McEwen, "Neuroscience, Molecular Biology, and the Childhood Roots of Health Disparities: Building a New Framework for Health Promotion and Disease Prevention," *JAMA: Journal of the American Medical Association* 301 (21) (June 2009), 2252–59.

123 disrupts the development of "brain architecture": Jack P. Shonkoff, "The Neurobiology of Early Childhood Development and the Foundation of a Sustainable Society," in *Investing Against Evidence: The Global State of Early Childhood Care and Education* (Paris: UNESCO, 2015).

123–24 the reduced "gray matter" in the cortex: Nicole L. Hair, Jamie L. Hanson, Barbara L. Wolfe, and Seth D. Pollak, "Association of Child Poverty, Brain Development, and Academic Achievement," *JAMA Pediatrics* 169 (9) (September 2015), 822–29.

124 A National Institutes of Health study based on MRIs: Clancy Blair and C. Cybele Raver, "Poverty, Stress, and Brain Development: New Directions for Prevention and Intervention," *Academic Pediatrics* 16 (3S) (April 2016), S30–S36.

125 15 percent less on schools in their poorest districts: Laura Bliss, "Watch Poverty in School Districts Escalate before Your Very Eyes," *CityLab*, August 26, 2015.

125 more than 50 percent of students in public schools in America: *A New Majority: Low-Income Students Now a Majority in the Nation's Public Schools* (Atlanta: Southern Education Foundation, 2015).

125 Only 8 percent of white students do: National Center for Education Statistics, "Percentage Distribution of Public School Students, By Student Race/Ethnicity and School Poverty Level: School Year 2015–16," *Fast Facts* (2018).

126 About 40 percent of all low-income children attend high-poverty schools: Tanvi Misra, "The Stark Inequality of U.S. Public Schools, Mapped," *CityLab*, May 14, 2015.

126 "the children who need the most are concentrated in schools least likely": Reed Jordan, "High-Poverty Schools

Undermine Education for Children of Color," *Urban Wire: The Blog of the Urban Institute* (May 19, 2015). See also Misra, "Stark Inequality."

126 a more accurate poverty line of $39,460 for a single-parent family: Data used for this computation were drawn from Office of the Assistant Secretary for Planning and Evaluation, "HHS Poverty Guidelines for 2019," aspe.hhs.gov (February 1, 2019).

126 The ten poorest public school districts in 2012: Michael B. Sauter, Thomas C. Frohlich, Samuel Stebbins, and Evan Comen, "Richest and Poorest School Districts," *24/7 Wall Street*, September 25, 2015.

127 One million children were not counted in the last national census: William P. O'Hare, Yeris Mayol-Garcia, Elizabeth Wildsmith, and Alicia Torres, *The Invisible Ones: How Latino Children Are Left Out of Our Nation's Census Count* (Bethesda, MD: Child Trends Hispanic Institute, 2016), 4.

128 there are three kinds of poverty lines: See Peter Townsend, *Poverty in the United Kingdom: A Survey of Household Resources and Standards of Living* (New York and Middlesex, UK: Penguin, 1979).

128 the nation needs an absolute poverty budget: See Tiago Mendonça dos Santos, "Poverty as Lack of Capabilities: An Analysis of the Definition of Poverty of Amartya Sen," *PERI* 9 (2) (2017), 107–24.

128 "Individuals, families, and groups in the population": Townsend, *Poverty in the United Kingdom*, 31.

129 their "household possessions, their housing, their neighborhoods": Kurt Bauman, Adam Carle, and Kathleen Short, "Accessing the Adult Wellbeing Topical Module in the Survey of Income and Program Participation (SIPP)," paper presented at the 29th General Conference of the International Association for Research in Income and Wealth (Joensuu, Finland, August 20–26, 2006), 17.

129 Sen's lists . . . included "being alive": Quoted in Wiebke

Kuklys and Ingrid Robeyns, "Sen's Capability Approach to Welfare Economics," paper presented to the Committee on Women, Population, and the Environment, *CWPE* 0415 (February 2004), 5.

131 "keep pace with mainstream living standards": Shawn Fremstad, *A Modern Framework for Measuring Poverty and Basic Economic Security* (Washington, DC: Center for Economic and Policy Research, 2010), 16.

131 Americans think the poverty line is around $33,000 a year: American Enterprise Institute and Los Angeles Times, *2016 Poverty Survey: Attitudes toward the Poor, Poverty, and Welfare in the United States* (Princeton, NJ: Princeton Survey Research Associates International, 2016), 7.

131 Fremstad computes that at 50 percent of median income: Fremstad, emails to the author, April 23 and 25, 2019.

132 Millions of people over time: Annie Carney, "Plan to Alter How Poverty Is Calculated by Census," *New York Times*, April 8, 2019, A18; Arloc Sherman and Paul M. Van de Water, "Reducing Cost-of-Living Adjustment Would Make Poverty Line a Less Accurate Measure of Basic Needs," (Washington, DC: Center for Budget and Policy Priorities, June 11, 2019).

CHAPTER 8: MONEY MATTERS

133 Recent research, however, has increasingly shown that low income itself is a key: See endnotes 9 and 10 to chapter 1, "Invisible Americans."

134 "household income appears to affect a wide range of different outcomes": Kerris Cooper and Kitty Stewart, *Does Money Affect Children's Outcomes? A Systematic Review* (York, UK: Joseph Rowntree Foundation, 2013), 37.

134 "through inadequate nutrition; fewer learning experiences": Brooks-Gunn and Duncan, "Effects of Poverty on Children," 56.

134 Newer research has focused on three pathways: Cooper and Stewart, *Does Money Affect Children's Outcomes?*, 45.

135 Money also helps reduce family stress: Ibid., 39.

135 Money also helps parents provide: Ibid.

135 the absence of money measurably affects poor children's ability: See endnote 5 to chapter 1, "Invisible Americans."

135 the longer children live below the poverty line: Robert L. Wagmiller Jr. and Robert M. Adelman, *Childhood and Intergenerational Poverty: The Long-Term Consequences of Growing Up Poor* (New York: National Center for Children in Poverty, 2009), 5, and Priyanka Boghani, "How Poverty Can Follow Children Into Adulthood," *Frontline*, PBS.org (November 22, 2017).

135 One in twenty live in poverty for ten years or more: Mark Greenberg, Indivar Dutta-Gupta, and Elisa Minoff, *From Poverty to Prosperity: A National Strategy to Cut Poverty in Half—Report and Recommendations of the Center for American Progress Task Force on Poverty* (Washington, DC: Center for American Progress, 2007), 2.

135 At age fifty, people who spent some time: See "Disease Prevalence at Age 50 Years, by Birth Weight and Childhood Socioeconomic Conditions: Panel Study of Income Dynamics, 1968–2007," in Rucker C. Johnson and Robert F. Schoeni, "Early-Life Origins of Adult Disease: National Longitudinal Population-Based Study of the United States," *American Journal of Public Health* 101 (12) (December 2011), 2317–24, 2320.

136 71 percent more likely to have a stroke or heart attack: Ibid.

136 "incomes are not as important to children's outcomes": Susan E. Mayer, *What Money Can't Buy: Family Income and Children's Life Chances* (Cambridge, MA: Harvard University Press, 1997), 2–3.

137 "statistically, the effects of maternal age": Brooks-Gunn and Duncan, "Effects of Poverty on Children," 56.

137–38 Those raised in periods when the family generally had more income: Greg J. Duncan, W. Jean Yeung, Jeanne Brooks-Gunn, and Judith R. Smith, "How Much Does Childhood Poverty Affect the Life Chances of Children?" *American Sociological Review* 63 (3) (June 1998), 406–23.

139 Researchers estimated how much improvement there was: See H. Luke Shaefer, Sophie Collyer, Greg Duncan, Kathryn Edin, Irwin Garfinkel, David Harris, Timothy M. Smeeding, et al., "A Universal Child Allowance: A Plan to Reduce Poverty and Income Instability among Children in the United States," 28.

139 One study also showed that the birth weight of newborns was higher: Kate W. Strully, David H. Rehkopf, and Ziming Xuan, "Effects of Prenatal Poverty on Infant Health: State Earned Income Tax Credits and Birth Weight," *American Sociological Review* 75 (4) (August 2010), 534–62.

139 It was a forerunner of the Earned Income Tax Credit: Thomas L. Hungerford and Rebecca Thiess, *The Earned Income Tax Credit and the Child Tax Credit: History, Purpose, Goals, and Effectiveness,* 2. See Robert J. Lampman, "Nixon's Family Assistance Plan," *Institute for Research on Poverty Discussion Paper* 57–69 (Madison: University of Wisconsin, 1969). See also John F. Cogan, "Labor Supply and Negative Income Taxation: New Evidence from the New Jersey-Pennsylvania Experiment," *Economic Inquiry* 21 (4) (October 1983), 465–84, and Robert A. Moffitt, "The Negative Income Tax: Would It Discourage Work?" *Monthly Labor Review* 104 (4) (April 1981), 23–27.

140 Each member of the Cherokee tribe was given a share: See Randall K. Q. Akee, William E. Copeland, Gordon Keeler, Adrian Angold, and Jane E. Costello, "Parents' Incomes and Children's Outcomes: A Quasi-Experiment Using Transfer Payments from Casino Profits," *American Economic Journal: Applied Economics* 2(1) (January 2010), 86–115. See also Robin J. Anderson, "Tribal Casino Impacts on American Indians' Well-Being: Evidence from

Reservation-Level Census Data," *Contemporary Economic Policy* 31 (2) (2013), 291–300, and Jonathan B. Taylor and Joseph P. Kalt, *American Indians on Reservations: A Databook of Socioeconomic Change between the 1990 and 2000 Censuses* (Cambridge, MA: Harvard Project on American Indian Economic Development, 2005).

141 Under the program, dubbed Mincome: David Calnitsky, "'More Normal than Welfare': The Mincome Experiment, Stigma, and Community Experience," *Canadian Review of Sociology* 53 (1) (February 2016), 26–71, and CBC News, "1970s Manitoba Poverty Experiment Called a Success," CBC.ca (March 25, 2010.) See also Evelyn L. Forget, "The Town with No Poverty: The Health Effects of a Canadian Guaranteed Annual Income Field Experiment," *Canadian Public Policy* 37 (3) (September 2011), 283–305, and Wayne Simpson, Greg Mason, and Ryan Godwin, "The Manitoba Basic Annual Income Experiment: Lessons Learned 40 Years Later," *Canadian Public Policy* 43 (1) (March 2017), 85–104.

142 Researchers found positive results: See Lauren E. Jones, Kevin S. Milligan, and Mark Stabile, "Child Cash Benefits and Family Expenditures: Evidence from the National Child Benefit," 1–41.

142 undertaken by the researchers at the London School of Economics: See Cooper and Stewart, *Does Money Affect Children's Outcomes?*

143 A summary published in 2016: Anna Aizer, Shari Eli, Joseph Ferrie, and Adriana Lleras-Muney, "The Long-Run Impact of Cash Transfers to Poor Families," *American Economic Review* 106 (4) (April 2016), 935–71.

144 According to one of the early surveys, low-income families spent: Greg J. Duncan and Richard J. Murnane, "Rising Inequality in Family Incomes and Children's Educational Outcomes," *RSF: The Russell Sage Foundation Journal of the Social Sciences* 2 (2) (May 2016), 145.

145 one-quarter of child maltreatment was attributable: See Dan Brown and Elisabetta De Cao, "The Impact of Unemployment on Child Maltreatment in the United States," *Department of Economics Discussion Paper Series* 837 (Oxford, UK: Oxford University, 2017).

145 increases in the EITC led to reduced child maltreatment: Lawrence M Berger, Sarah A. Font, Kristen S. Slack, and Jane Waldfogel, "Income and Child Maltreatment in Unmarried Families: Evidence from the Earned Income Tax Credit," *Review of Economics of the Household* 15 (4) (December 2017), 1345–72.

145 when income increased, parents spent more on children's clothing, toys: See Paul Gregg, Jane Waldfogel, and Elizabeth Washbrook, "Family Expenditures Post–Welfare Reform in the UK: Are Low-Income Families Starting to Catch Up?" *Labour Economics* 13 (6) (December 2006), 721– 46.

145 "we come to several major conclusions": Hirokazu Yoshi-kawa, J. Lawrence Aber, and William Beardslee, "The Effects of Poverty on the Mental, Emotional, and Behav-ioral Health of Children and Youth: Implications for Pre-vention," *American Psychologist* (May-June 2012), 272–84.

146 half the achievement gap could be closed: Cooper and Stewart, *Does Money Affect Children's Outcomes?*, 35.

CHAPTER 9: THE BEHAVIOR OF THE POOR IS NOT THE PRIORITY

147 the source of poverty often pivots around poor unwed mothers: See Isabel V. Sawhill and Ron Haskins, *Work and Marriage: The Way to End Poverty and Welfare* (Washington, DC: Brookings Institution, 2003).

148 "no government program is likely to reduce child poverty as much as": Isabel Sawhill, "20 Years Later, It Turns Out Dan Quayle Was Right about Murphy Brown and Unmarried Moms," *Washington Post*, May 25, 2012.

148 Even Sawhill concedes, "For women under age 30": Ibid.

148 another related possibility for unmarried births: George A. Akerlof and Janet L. Yellen, *An Analysis of Out-of-Wedlock Births in the United States* (Washington, DC: Brookings Institution, 1996).

149 "The growth in the rate of unmarried births in the United States": Peter Edelman, *So Rich, So Poor: Why It's So Hard to End Poverty in America* (New York: New Press, 2013), 38.

150 such a comparison in 2017: David, Ryan M. Finnigan, and Sabine Hübgen, "Rethinking the Risks of Poverty: A Framework for Analyzing Prevalences and Penalties," *American Journal of Sociology*, November 2017, 740–86.

150 "Scholars routinely ask why the poor fail to get married": Ibid., 770.

150 As for single-female-headed families: Ibid., 750.

151 "The proportion of [American] children living with a single mother": Patrick Heuveline and Matthew Weinshenker, "The International Poverty Gap: Does Demography Matter?" *Demography* 45 (1) (February 2008), 173–91, 179.

151 "If you lack a high school degree": David Brady, Ryan M. Finnigan, and Sabine Hübgen, "Single Mothers Are Not the Problem," *New York Times*, February 10, 2018.

152 "we had stumbled onto a major social change": PBS, "Daniel Patrick Moynihan Interview," PBS.org (2001).

153 "Among parents living below the poverty line": Shawn Fremstad, *Married . . . without Means: Poverty and Economic Hardship Among Married Americans* (Washington, DC: Center for Economic and Policy Research, 2012), 1.

153 "The problem is that there's no evidence": Quoted in Emily Badger, "It's Time to Stop Blaming Poverty on the Decline in Marriage," *CityLab*, January 8, 2014.

CHAPTER 10: WHAT TO DO

156 Austria, Belgium, Bulgaria, Canada: Horacio Levy, Manos Matsaganis, and Holly Sutherland, "Towards a European

Union Child Basic Income? Within and Between Country Effects," *International Journal of Microsimulation* 6 (1) (2013), 64.

156 As of 2016, Canada had a base child allowance of $4,935: See "Canada Child Benefit," Canada.ca (April 17, 2018).

156 The benefit for two children in Brussels . . . and in Germany: See "Child Benefit Calculator," MyFamily.be (May 4, 2019), and "How to Calculate Child Benefit ('Kindergeld') in Germany," lawyerdb.de (May 4, 2019).

156 in Ireland . . . and in the Netherlands: See "Child Benefit," CitizensInformation.ie (March 26, 2019), and "Child Benefit: How Much Child Benefit Will You Get?" SVB.nl (May 4, 2019).

157 increases in spending on children's needs: Gregg, Waldfogel, and Washbrook, "Family Expenditures Post–Welfare Reform in the UK," 721–46.

157 the money mostly went to work-related expenses: Neeraj Kaushal, Qin Gao, and Jane Waldfogel, "Welfare Reform and Family Expenditures: How Are Single Mothers Adapting to the New Welfare and Work Regime?" *Social Science Review* 81 (3), 369–96.

157 Conservatives . . . prefer reducing government's patronizing control: See Samuel Hammond and Robert Orr, *Toward a Universal Child Benefit* (Washington, DC: Niskanen Center, 2016).

158 an annual cash grant of $10,000 a year to Americans over twenty-one: Charles Murray, *In Our Hands: A Plan to Replace the Welfare State* (Washington, DC: AEI Press, 2006).

158 free, public, and compulsory primary education: Michael S. Katz, *A History of Compulsory Education Laws* (Bloomington, IN: Phi Delta Kappa Educational Foundation, 1976).

158 an unconditional child allowance, in contrast to many of those in Latin America: See Laura G. Dávila Lárraga, *How Does Prospera Work? Best Practices in the Implementation of Conditional Cash Transfer Programs in Latin America and*

the Caribbean (Washington, DC: Inter-American Development Bank, 2016).

159 "Washington has spent trillions of dollars on dozens of programs": Quoted in Robert Greenstein, *Welfare Reform and the Safety Net: Evidence Contradicts Likely Assumptions behind Forthcoming GOP Poverty Plan* (Washington, DC: Center on Budget and Policy Priorities, 2016).

159 social programs have at most a minor influence on Americans' willingness to work: See Robert Moffitt, "An Economic Model of Welfare Stigma," *American Economic Review* 73 (5) (December 1983), 1023–35. See also Sherman, Greenstein, and Ruffing, *Contrary to "Entitlement Society" Rhetoric.*

159 The Trump White House economists produced a poverty report: Council of Economic Advisers, *Expanding Work Requirements in Non-Cash Welfare Programs* (Washington, DC: Executive Office of the President of the United States, 2018).

159 60 percent of the recipients had full- or part-time jobs: Rachel Garfield, Robin Rudowitz, and Anthony Damico, *Understanding the Intersection of Medicaid and Work* (San Francisco: Henry J. Kaiser Family Foundation, 2018).

159 cash allowances in more than half a dozen developing nations: Abhijit Banerjee, Rema Hanna, Gabriel Kreindler, and Benjamin A. Olken, *Debunking the Stereotype of the Lazy Welfare Recipient: Evidence from Cash Transfer Programs Worldwide* (Cambridge, MA: Poverty Action Lab, 2015).

160 "between 1995 . . . and 2005 . . . , the share of children in deep poverty rose": Greenstein, *Welfare Reform and the Safety Net,* 3.

160 had seemingly put to rest claims that welfare led to destructive dependencies: See Mary Corcoran, Greg J. Duncan, Gerald Gurin, and Patricia Gurin, "Myth and Reality: The Causes and Persistence of Poverty," *Journal of Policy Analysis and Management* 4 (4) (Summer 1985), 516–36.

160 used a different methodology: Mary Jo Bane and David T. Ellwood, "Slipping Into and Out of Poverty: The Dynamics of Spells," *National Bureau of Economic Research Working Paper* 1199 (September 1983).

161 jobs taken due to TANF often paid low wages: See Fredrik Andersson, Julia Lane, and Erika McEntarfer, *Successful Transitions out of Low-Wage Work for Temporary Assistance for Needy Families (TANF) Recipients: The Role of Employers, Coworkers, and Location* (Washington, DC: U.S. Department of Health and Human Services, 2004). See also Greg Kaufmann, "This Week in Poverty: Revealing the Real TANF," *The Nation* (February 8, 2013), and Alana Semuels, "The Near Impossibility of Moving Up after Welfare," *The Atlantic* (July 11, 2016).

162 a project called Sure Start: Neal Halfon, "Poverty, Complexity, and a New Way Forward," *Academic Pediatrics* 16 (3S) (April 2016), S16–S18.

162 In the UK, the child poverty rate before figuring in government programs and taxes: Janet C. Gornick and Emily Nell, "Children, Poverty, and Public Policy," *Luxembourg Income Study Working Papers* 701 (December 2017).

163 "Irrespective of their professed commitment to young children": Halfon, "Poverty, Complexity," x.

164 required parents to meet education and healthcare standards: Melisa Handl and Susan Spronk, "With Strings Attached," *Jacobin* (November 24, 2015).

164 ten alternative policies involving different levels of cash allowances: Irwin Garfinkel, David Harris, Jane Waldfogel, and Christopher Wimer, *Doing More for Our Children: Modeling a Universal Child Allowance or More Generous Child Tax Credit* (New York: Century Foundation and Bernard L. Schwartz Rediscovering Government Initiative, 2016).

165 if a $2,500 annual cash disbursement was provided for every child in America: Ibid., 2.

165 In the most generous program tested, a $4,000: Ibid., 12.

166 A respected group of child poverty economists: See H. Luke Shaefer, Sophie Collyer, Greg Duncan, Kathryn Edin, Irwin Garfinkel, David Harris, Timothy M. Smeeding, et al., "A Universal Child Allowance: A Plan to Reduce Poverty and Income Instability among Children in the United States." Ibid., 33.

167 the scholars' proposal of $3,000 a year: Ibid., 36.

168 A still newer set of programs, including child cash allowances: Greg Duncan and Suzanne Le Menestrel, eds., *A Roadmap to Reducing Child Poverty* (Washington, DC: National Academies of Sciences, Engineering, and Medicine, 2019).

EPILOGUE: FAITH IN THE POOR

170 A bill was proposed by Senators Michael Bennett and Sherrod Brown: Dylan Matthews, "Senate Democrats Have a Plan That Could Cut Child Poverty Nearly in Half," *Vox* (October 26, 2017).

171 Sen believes "poverty is unfreedom": Alicja Gescinska, "Poverty Is Unfreedom," *Brussels Times,* November 27, 2016.

INDEX

Page numbers in *italics* refer to figures and tables.

ALSO BY
JEFF MADRICK

SEVEN BAD IDEAS
How Mainstream Economists Have Damaged
America and the World

Ideas have the power to change history. But what happens when they are bad? In a tour de force of economics, history, and analysis, Jeff Madrick shows how theories on austerity, inflation, and efficient markets have become unassailable mantras over recent years, to the detriment of the country as a whole. Working backwards from the Great Recession, Madrick pulls no punches as he reconsiders seven of the greatest false idols of modern economic theory, from Say's law to Milton Friedman, illustrating how these ideas have been damaging markets, infrastructure, and individual livelihoods for years. Trenchant, sweeping, and empirical, *Seven Bad Ideas* resoundingly disrupts the status quo of modern economic theory.

Business

ALSO AVAILABLE
Age of Greed

VINTAGE BOOKS
Available wherever books are sold.
www.vintagebooks.com